REAL CONFIDENCE

Stop feeling small and start being brave

PSYCHOLOGIES
MAGAZINE

This edition first published 2016

© 2016 Kelsey Publishing Limited

Registered office

John Wiley and Sons Ltd, The Atrium, Southern Gate, Chichester, West Sussex, PO19 8SQ, United Kingdom

For details of our global editorial offices, for customer services and for information about how to apply for permission to reuse the copyright material in this book please see our website at www.wiley.com.

The right of the author to be identified as the author of this work has been asserted in accordance with the Copyright, Designs and Patents Act 1988.

Reprinted March 2016

Wiley publishes in a variety of print and electronic formats and by print-on-demand. Some material included with standard print versions of this book may not be included in e-books or in print-on-demand. If this book refers to media such as a CD or DVD that is not included in the version you purchased, you may download this material at http:// booksupport.wiley.com. For more information about Wiley products, visit www.wiley.com.

Designations used by companies to distinguish their products are often claimed as trademarks. All brand names and product names used in this book and on its cover are trade names, service marks, trademarks or registered trademarks of their respective owners. The publisher and the book are not associated with any product or vendor mentioned in this book. None of the companies referenced within the book have endorsed the book. Some names and identifying details have been changed to protect the privacy of individuals.

Limit of Liability/Disclaimer of Warranty: While the publisher and author have used their best efforts in preparing this book, they make no representations or warranties with respect to the accuracy or completeness of the contents of this book and specifically disclaim any implied warranties of merchantability or fitness for a particular purpose. It is sold on the understanding that the publisher is not engaged in rendering professional services and neither the publisher nor the author shall be liable for damages arising herefrom. If professional advice or other expert assistance is required, the services of a competent professional should be sought.

Library of Congress Cataloging-in-Publication Data is available

A catalogue record for this book is available from the British Library.

ISBN 978-0-857-08657-0 (pbk)
ISBN 978-0-857-08658-7 (ebk)   ISBN 978-0-857-08659-4 (ebk)

Cover design: Wiley

Set in 9/12pt ITC Franklin Gothic Std by Aptara

Printed in Great Britain by TJ International Ltd, Padstow, Cornwall, UK

CONTENTS

FOREWORD

by Suzy Greaves, Editor, Psychologies

When I'm out and about meeting and hanging out with our *Psychologies* readers at our events and festivals, we often talk about no-limits, 'magic wand' thinking. If you could wave a wand and could change something about yourself – what would you change? 'Confidence' is the word I hear over and over again. Deep down we believe that if we could only be a little bit more confident and comfortable in our own skin, the world would be our oyster ... we could do anything ... the sky would be the limit. But because we're not confident, we can't. So we sit quietly and leave it to those confident people over there to conquer the world and reach for the sky.

So if that is your belief, this book may very well change your life – as well as challenge you quite a bit. Because this book is going to invite you to be brave. You will be relieved (I was!) to discover that it's normal – and healthy – to feel scared when you're about to do something new – be it a new role at work, a first date or learning a new skill. And you will learn that the only way to overcome your fears is by being brave. This book will show you how – from overcoming your initial fears to just 'having a go' until you become more skilled – as you slowly take baby steps out of your comfort zone. Then, over time, you can build your confidence on a foundation of real skill and faith in your ability versus that dreadful 'I feel a fraud' dread that haunts your every move. Courage and striving for accomplishment is the secret to real confidence – and I'm delighted that even though you're scared, you've been brave enough to pick up this book and come on this journey with us. No more sitting quietly over there, it's time to conquer the world and reach for the sky.

Ready?

Suzy Greaves, Editor, *Psychologies*

INTRODUCTION

Y ou might be surprised to know this, but buying a book about confidence is in fact a sign of confidence. At *Psychologies* magazine we believe that confidence begins with self-awareness, knowing exactly who you are and how you are in different life situations.

Right now you've identified that finding real confidence is what you need. Perhaps you might be aware that chronic low confidence is at the root of all your problems. Or perhaps you lack confidence in one particular area in your life – maybe you shine at work but want to disappear behind the curtains at social events. There might be just one particular fear like public speaking that you'd like to find the confidence for.

Whatever your reasons are for buying this book, one thing is for sure: you're not alone. Although there aren't any official statistics on people suffering from lack of confidence we know that it's a huge preoccupation for people. We know this from our readership research, from what psychologists, psychotherapists, life coaches and all the experts we talk to tell us. We know that people are Googling confidence, self-confidence, how to be confident and every variation. That's why we decided to create this book for you, providing all the latest research and the best expert knowledge in one handy book. We've done the research for you and formulated our philosophy so that you have a clear understanding of what to do next.

What we hope this book will do for you is help you understand what confidence really is while showing you how to develop confidence for real. Understanding why you lack confidence is of course important, but we're not going to dwell on that too much. We believe it's good to understand why we are the way we are, but we know that you've bought this book because you want to leave the past behind and become the best you. If you didn't believe this was possible, you wouldn't be reading this – and that in itself is a sign of confidence.

You've probably read or been told that you should fake it until you make it, that you should *act* confident. But think of your favourite actors and why you love them and one of the main reasons is that whichever character they play they are totally believable. They don't appear to be 'acting'.

Our approach to confidence is based on not acting. We want you to feel relaxed in absolutely any situation and accept who you are. We want to show you that confidence has nothing to do with any type of personality and that what you may think of as confidence is often a fake front, arrogance or narcissism. And that's not the person you want to be. Having a go at what you find difficult, slowly trying and going step by baby step, staying on track, being patient and focused on developing different skills is what real confidence is.

HOW TO USE THIS BOOK

We've divided this book into three parts (How Confident Are You? Why Do You Lack Confidence? How Can You Learn to be Confident?). In Part 1 you'll gain a sense of how low your confidence really is by understanding the true meaning of confidence. You may indeed discover you're not so bad after all. In Part 2 you'll explore why you are the way you are, which will help you move on. Finally, in Part 3 we have lots of practical advice. To help you take immediate action we also have confidence boosters throughout the book so that you can work on your confidence immediately.

At the end of the first five chapters there are tests that will help you assess yourself. There are also key 'Ask Yourself' questions at the end of each chapter for you to reflect on so that you can relate each chapter to your personal experience. You will also find case studies, who are all real people (with names and identifying circumstances changed). Their journeys will help you see how it's possible to overcome low confidence.

We interviewed two psychologists, two acting coaches, two life coaches and one neuroscientist, all of them top of their fields, and the best experts on confidence. Instead of just one perspective we wanted to tackle every aspect and show you how experts from different areas converge. We wanted to create a *Psychologies* perspective on Real Confidence that is multidimensional, giving you an all-round, thorough approach. We hope that through this you are able to stop seeing lack of confidence as a problem that is an obstacle to your happiness.

OUR EXPERTS

Annie Ashdown, Harley Street business and personal development coach, clinical hypnotherapist, and intuitive

Ashdown's clients include CEOs, lawyers, entrepreneurs, diplomats, doctors, corporate employees, top achievers in business, celebrities and teenagers. She is the author of *Doormat Nor Diva Be – How to Take Back Control of your Life and Relationships* (Infinite Ideas) and *The Confidence Factor – 7 Secrets of Successful People* (Crimson Publishing).

www.annieashdown.com
@Annie_Ashdown

Dr Ilona Boniwell, founder of the European Network of Positive Psychology, head of the International MSc in Applied Positive Psychology at Anglia Ruskin University (UK and France) and head of training consultancy Positran

Boniwell has been involved in helping the government of Bhutan develop a framework for happiness-based public policy. She has contributed to, edited and written several books. Her latest as an author is *Oxford Handbook of Happiness* (Oxford University Press) and positive psychology tools, such as Strength Cards and The Happiness Box (Positran).

www.positran.co.uk

Dawn Breslin, life coach, TV presenter and author

Breslin's extensive TV work includes presenter and confidence-building expert for GMTV, and presenter for Discovery Channel's *Life Coach* Series. She helps people from all walks of life repair their self-esteem and rebuild their confidence. She is the author of three books, *Zest for Life*, *Super Confidence* and *The Power Book* (Hay House) and was a consultant on Lorraine Kelly's book, *Real Life Solutions* (Century).

www.dawnbreslin.com
@DawnBreslin01

Dr Nitasha Buldeo, research scientist in biophysiology

Buldeo is qualified in health sciences and psychology, neuroscience, nutrition and NLP. As a product-innovator and entrepreneur she has been awarded scholarships from the UK Department of Trade and Industry to study at the Kellogg School of Management in Chicago, USA. She was also awarded a scholarship at business school, Cranfield School of Management.

www.nitashabuldeo.com
@NitashaBuldeo

Dr Tomas Chamorro-Premuzic, Psychologist and Professor of Business Psychology at University College London and Columbia University, CEO of Hogan Assessment Systems (psychological profiling)

Chamorro-Premuzic advises clients in financial services, media, consumer, fashion and government and appears regularly on news channels including the BBC, CNN and Sky. He is the author of eight books, including his latest *Confidence: The Surprising Truth About How Much You Need and How to Get It* (Profile Books).

www.drtomascp.com
@drtcp

Niki Flacks, award-winning veteran Broadway actress, director, acting/corporate training coach, psychologist, therapist, founder of the Bergerac Company

Flacks, also a former assistant professor in theatre at Southern Methodist University, fuses psychology and neuroscience to help actors handle nerves and create authentic characters. Her flagship programme for corporations is Power Talk, which trains employees in overcoming fear of public speaking. She is the author of *Acting with Passion* (Bloomsbury Methuen Drama).

www.nikiflacks.com
www.bergeracco.com/
@NikiFlacksAct

Patsy Rodenburg OBE, Head of Voice at the Guildhall School of Music and Drama, leadership coach

Rodenburg was former Head of Voice at the Royal National Theatre, and works with the Royal Shakespeare Company, the Royal Court, the Donmar and Almeida theatres, as well as A-list stars. She travels all over the world coaching business leaders, athletes and politicians. She is the author of five books including *Presence* (Penguin).

www.patsyrodenburg.com

1 HOW CONFIDENT ARE YOU?

CHAPTER 1

DEFINING CONFIDENCE – IS IT WHAT YOU THINK IT IS?

W e suspect you believe lack of confidence is the reason certain aspects of your life are not working out the way they do for everyone else who has confidence. You don't blame anyone else for not earning more money, or not finding a job post-redundancy, or not finding love after divorce, or not buying a home, or not having children, or not changing careers, or not losing weight, or not getting fit, or not making new friends. This feeling, that it's *your* fault, that it's all because you've got no confidence, is very common. You're not alone. Lacking confidence doesn't feel good. You feel like there's some screw missing from the intricate parts of your brain, or there's a malfunction in your brain's software, right? If you could just fix that, if there was a confidence app for your brain you'd be fine, right?

Confidence has become the holy grail of modern life. It's not just the big concepts like success and happiness that we've come to believe *depend* on confidence, somehow we think that it's the foundation to our inner structure, that it's what would enable us to create our ideal outer lives.

But do we even know what it *really* is? Unless you really know what confidence is, how can you develop it? What *is* it?

Analysing the meaning of confidence prompts fascinating discussions. Let's start with the *Oxford English Dictionary* definition. Here we see that one aspect of the meaning is a feeling of *being able to trust or rely on someone or something*. That's a reminder that we need to learn to trust and rely on ourselves. (If you already trust and rely on yourself, even just a little, then you can smile and feel good about yourself.)

As for the definition with regard to individuals, the following comes up in the *Oxford Advanced Learner's Dictionary*:

A feeling of self-assurance arising from an appreciation of one's own abilities or qualities.

A belief in your own ability to do something and be successful.

The feeling that you are certain about something.

Specifying 'self-confidence' gives us the following dictionary definition:

A feeling of trust in one's abilities, qualities and judgement.

If we also look at the *Oxford English Dictionary* definition of self-esteem, it seems to be one step further than confidence in our own worth or abilities:

A feeling of being happy with your own character and abilities.

So is confidence based on self-esteem? Is self-esteem inner and confidence outer, or does outer confidence show inner self-esteem? Does high self-esteem lead to self-confidence? What a mental maze.

FINDING A PERSONAL DEFINITION

Social psychology studies have shown that we try to manage our feelings of self-worth. With social media, and generations who haven't experienced life without social media, there is a whole new arena to research. A University of Wisconsin and Madison[1] 2013 study measuring Facebook users' self-esteem looked at how quickly participants made positive associations about themselves when looking at their own profile. But the study didn't look at how and why a Facebook profile is a version of self, or to what extent it's a *true* version. If Photoshopped and filtered photos boost your self-esteem, then how real is it? If you've posted photos from parties where it looks as though you're having a fabulous time, but in reality you left early because your ex was there or you were bored, how does looking at photos of yourself looking good help you *feel* good at the next party or when you're on your own?

The above study didn't assess the effect of people looking at other people's profiles and newsfeeds. One that did was the 2014 study at the University of Queensland's School of Psychology,[2] which found that active participation in social media produces a positive sense of belonging. The study looked at one group of people in which half posted regularly on Facebook while the other half passively observed posts. According to the study, not posting for two days had a negative effect on those who were simply observing the posts. In another group, participants using anonymous accounts were encouraged to respond to each other. However, half of the group were unaware they were set up not to receive any responses. Those who didn't receive responses felt invisible with lower self-esteem. What does this tell us about self-esteem? That it's changeable, that it's vulnerable, that it's dependent on the group and peer activity? And how does this all tie up with confidence?

If you're someone who receives compliments about how together you are, if you can be the joker of the group, or if your job involves helping others at a high level, and yet lack of confidence is your guilty secret, then you know all too well that appearances are deceptive. If you can appear to be confident to others but aren't inside, what does this mean? How can we define confidence to take these contradictions into account?

Enter the academics, with a term we don't use every day: self-efficacy. In the good old *Oxford English Dictionary*, efficacy is defined as *the ability of something to produce the results that are wanted* whilst self-efficacy is *the ability to produce a desire or intended result*.

Let's say you want to start going to a yoga class to de-stress. You've put it off because you feel hopeless at anything new, you don't like group activities and you don't like your body in gym clothes. In short your self-esteem is low. But finally, out of desperation to help you sleep, you go to a low-key class that a neighbour has recommended. Everyone is friendly, no one is in scary designer gear, no one is looking at anyone, you forget yourself and time, and during relaxation you go out like a light, and come round at the end of the class feeling refreshed. You've produced your intended result.

If we can change our personal definition of confidence, could that change our view of confidence? If you were totally clear about what confidence is, would it be less elusive and more attainable?

CONFIDENCE MEANS HAVING A GO

One of the problems with defining confidence is that the psychologists themselves haven't researched this much. Most of the research is somewhere between self-esteem and self-efficacy. Self-efficacy is a concept that first emerged in the 1970s through Canadian psychologist Albert Bandura[3] and has been researched extensively.

66 Self-esteem is more about liking yourself. Self-efficacy is our belief in our capacity to try and accomplish something. 99

Dr Ilona Boniwell, positive psychologist

If you don't like yourself it's not easy to change this. If you don't like a part of yourself, it's not easy to change this. Let's say you don't like your body. You might very well find the idea of going to a gym intimidating because you picture that it will be full of people perfecting their six-packs and toned bodies. But you might decide to give running a try because you live near a splendid park and were pretty good at running at school. You discover it clears your head after work, you get fit and then proudly notice your body looking better.

Bandura's definition of self-efficacy in simple terms means: 'I can have a go. I'm hopeless at exercise, I've been a couch potato for years, but I was good at running at school, so I might like it again. I can give it a try and see how I get on.' What this shows is that confidence is a skill that can be learnt, as long as we simply try.

66 *I can have a go* is not a guarantee of a positive outcome, but it's a positive feeling that you are able to try. 99

Dr Ilona Boniwell, positive psychologist

What Boniwell highlights is that there's confusion and misrepresentation in our society as to what confidence actually is. People with inflated self-esteem might have real confidence, but they might not. While self-esteem applies to our character in general, self-efficacy is what explains why we can be confident in one area of our lives and not in another.

DR ILONA BONIWELL ON DEVELOPING CONFIDENCE IN DIFFERENT AREAS

Boniwell, a highly qualified academic and accomplished professional, remembers being confident at school from the start. 'Very early on I was confident reading poems in front of hundreds of pupils. I was always confident with teachers.' But as the tallest girl (she was her adult height at the age of 12) she had to contend with all the other children at school making fun of her. When her family moved from Latvia to Saransk, Russia, she was the tallest female in a city of 300,000 people. 'I was called giraffe. And Eiffel Tower.'

As a result of her height she wasn't confident with boys. For a start she had to wait for them to catch up with her height. By the time she was 19 her confidence began to develop but she admits it wasn't until her late 20s that she got over this. Her personal experience underlines her views on confidence: 'We can be confident in one thing and not another. And we can develop confidence in areas where we lack confidence. That was the case with me.'

Looking at definitions of confidence and delving into what it means as a word and an academic term in psychology, as well as in actual living terms, immediately makes it more accessible. Self-esteem might be a part of confidence, but it's by no means the only part. That's great news because changing self-esteem is much harder work, but by developing confidence, your self-esteem will increase too. Reading this book shows that you are willing to give something new a go and you're prepared to try advice offered to you – and this willingness to try is a crucial part of confidence.

Of course, when we think of confidence we tend to think of a certain stand-out quality. Confident people shine, don't they?

EVERYONE HAS THE 'IT' FACTOR

> **"Confidence is being fully present. Confidence is what some people call the 'it' factor."**

Patsy Rodenburg, OBE, voice and leadership coach

When we refer to celebrities as stars it's because we of course believe that stars shine big time. You may be thinking that mere mortals surely cannot attain the 'it' factor possessed by stars. Yet according to Patsy Rodenburg, who is sought after by the biggest acting stars, every one of us is born with 'presence'. Though it can get lost, it's reassuring that Rodenburg absolutely insists that every one of us can re-engage this 'it' factor.

What might come as a surprise is what contributes to this 'it' factor or what can ignite it. For Rodenburg, who also coaches leaders and athletes, real confidence comes from deep knowledge, but she points out that this isn't fashionable at the moment in our society. And of course we know she's right. Anyone can be an expert on anything by Googling something. If you are suffering from chronic low confidence you might even have come to the conclusion that confidence *is* superficial knowledge but, as you'll discover, *real* confidence is far from superficial. Rodenburg always goes back to the Ancient Greeks to make her point about self-awareness. Carved on the tree before they visited the oracle were the words Know Thy Self. Knowing yourself means accepting gaps of knowledge and gaining knowledge – which will provide you with confidence. We're told that knowledge is power but it's way more important than that – it generates that 'it' factor.

One of the problems with defining confidence is that because it's complex, identifying it in others is not straightforward. It's tempting to assume that anyone who appears fearless is confident. But would they describe themselves as such?

CONFIDENCE IS IN THE EYES OF THE BEHOLDER

> **"When we are confident in doing something, it tends to be afterwards that we realize this. That's when we say WOW I really did that, I was confident."**

Niki Flacks, acting coach, psychologist, therapist

We may think performers are the people who personify confidence because they put themselves up in front of an audience with the fear of forgetting what they have memorized and the risk of negative responses. Yet former Broadway actress Niki Flacks points out that actors on stage can be having a wonderful time, but feel awful backstage. They may have been shaking with nerves and pacing up and down to the toilet beforehand, but then they step on stage relaxed and forget their nerves.

The reason for this, as Flacks explains, is that when people are *doing* in the moment they are not *thinking* confident, and this is exactly the case with actors and other performers on stage. It's important to remember that the same applies to many situations where you would like to acquire confidence. You might be admiring the colleague who is great at business pitches, or the friend who cooks gourmet dinners for large groups, but they may not be thinking of themselves as confident. They might have had a lot of practice (in turn, gaining a huge amount of knowledge), and love what they do. They too might still have a flurry of nerves before a business presentation, or before 20 people arrive for dinner. The point is you don't have to wait for that magical day to feel confident to do what you dream of. Simply try to do it, and the magic will follow.

PAY ATTENTION TO NATURE

When you're feeling less than good about yourself, one of the easiest ways to take the negative focus away is to target your thoughts at nature. Simply noticing the flowers blooming in your pot plant, the changing colours of the leaves on the trees in your street, the smell of freshness after the rain, can begin to transform your outlook.

Is there a park near your workplace or home? Can you walk home from work via parks and canals and leafy back streets? Can you go on daytrips at the weekend somewhere not too far but wild and wonderful? Is there a beach where you can walk on the sand or the pebbles? Walking outside surrounded by nature will help you feel alive in your body, and that will boost your mood no end.

CONFIDENCE IS MULTI-DIMENSIONAL

> **"One minute we're talking to someone and we feel great, the next we're talking to someone else and it's gone. "**

Niki Flacks, acting coach, psychologist, therapist

One of the reasons that confidence is a tricky term to define and apply to our lives is that it's changeable. It's important to realize, expect, and accept that not only will confidence vary from one area of our lives to another, it can shift at different times. Knowing this is the case means you won't be unrealistic in how you visualize confidence. As Flacks underlines, we can be confident one moment and not the next, and this is entirely normal.

If you think of confidence as an attitude that embraces several dimensions then it becomes less abstract. It's likely that you can find at least one dimension that applies to you, one element that you can own and feel good about, and you can even unravel why your confidence shifts.

Confidence coach Annie Ashdown's book *The Confidence Factor* outlines the seven habits of the confident: self-respect, self-approval, self-worth, self-mastery, self-belief, self-responsibility, self-assertiveness. Even if you are at your lowest point right now and want to say that none of these apply to you, the fact that you are reading this demonstrates that you have the habit of self-responsibility. In short, this means you can get out of how you feel right now.

> **"Confidence enables a positive perception of one's self and abilities and is demonstrated by a robust sense of belief, self-assurance, courageous vulnerability, assertiveness, humility, optimism and enthusiasm."**
>
> Annie Ashdown, confidence coach

Relating a definition of confidence to yourself, who you are and how you feel is crucial. This book is called *Real Confidence* because it has to feel real to you. Life coach Dawn Breslin began to adapt her definition of confidence the more she worked with people who had lost their confidence as a result of some sort of life event. Her original definition of confidence was about the removal of self-doubt, and the by-product of healthy self-esteem and healthy self-belief – which felt like a stock explanation. She then realized her work as a confidence coach became a process of reminding clients from all walks of life who they really are.

"Confidence is not projecting or trying to be. It's about trusting yourself and knowing you can live the way you want to live."

Dawn Breslin, confidence coach

We've spent time analysing the definition of confidence so that we can dispel any fairy tales you've created about it. We hope you're relieved to hear that real confidence is not really about outward appearances but about an inner decision to simply try and accomplish something. It's not about looking as if you're an expert, it's about taking the time to gain the knowledge that turns you into a true expert. It's a trust in your ability to try. It's more than likely that you're confident in one area in your life, even if you don't realize you are. When you do something you love or know a lot about, you don't *think* confident, you just *do*. We're going to be nudging you to do more doing than thinking because that's what leads to confidence. We're all born with the 'it' quality, it's just that life gets in the way.

We hope that this book will help you get back to who you feel you really are and how you want to live your life.

ASK YOURSELF

Q What has confidence meant for you so far?

Q Can you identify areas in your life where you are confident now?

Q What positive comments do you receive? (Even if you find it difficult to accept these, write them down.)

Q What stops you from focusing on positive rather than negative comments towards you?

Q Will you think of confidence in a different way now?

HOW CONFIDENT ARE YOU?

How confident do you feel on a day to day basis? If lacking self-confidence, we often devalue ourselves in the eyes of others, and sometimes even put ourselves down. Conversely, having too much can make us look self-satisfied and arrogant. How confident do you feel? How confident would other people think you are? How can you be sure of yourself without overdoing it? Here are 12 questions to assess your confidence, and, depending on your result, help you find the right balance.

Test by Philip Carter and Ken Russell
Translated by Nora Mahony

QUESTION 1

Would you appear on a television game show?

A. Yes
B. I don't know
C. No

QUESTION 2

Giving a long speech at your best friend's wedding wouldn't embarrass you at all.

A. Yes
B. I don't know
C. No

QUESTION 3

Are you a particularly positive person?

A. Yes
B. I don't know
C. No

QUESTION 4

Would you like to pilot an aeroplane?

A. Yes
B. I don't know
C. No

QUESTION 5

Would you like to meet royalty?

A. Yes
B. I don't know
C. No

QUESTION 6

Have you ever disagreed with your boss at work?

A. Yes

B. I don't know

C. No

QUESTION 7

Being naked in front of your friends doesn't bother you.

A. Yes

B. I don't know

C. No

QUESTION 8

Would you contradict a traffic warden if you thought you were in the right?

A. Yes

B. I don't know

C. No

QUESTION 9

Do you think that attack is the best form of defence?

A. Yes

B. I don't know

C. No

QUESTION 10

Driving in bad traffic doesn't bother you.

A. Yes

B. I don't know

C. No

QUESTION 11

Do you feel confident while crossing the road?

A. Yes

B. I don't know

C. No

QUESTION 12

Would you take the ferry if it were stormy?

A. Yes

B. I don't know

C. No

Mainly As:

You're sure of what you're doing.

You are the right person to have around when the stakes are high. You like to get involved in everything that happens around you. For example, if your department had to be completely restructured, you would want to be involved in the reorganization process in order to make a good impression – or even to secure a better position for yourself. In a similar situation, a less confident person would be unnerved by the changes to come or fear a wave of layoffs or the redefinition of his or her position. But be careful not to show too much confidence in yourself or to overestimate your abilities, as this might lead you to take unnecessary risks or to be seen as arrogant or smug by the people close to you. Remember that success is earned, not ordered.

Mainly Bs:

You believe in yourself enough for other people to trust you.

You are relatively self-confident and you are ready to take calculated risks in order to succeed. But you still prefer security and you avoid excessive risks. Even if you are confident in your abilities, you make sure not to be excessively so, and always make your decisions after thinking through all the options. Stay aware of your attitude to risk and keep trying to inch yourself out of your comfort zone in non-threatening situations so you can build a stronger capacity for dealing with any fears. Get comfortable with failing as well as succeeding. This will build your confidence in being able to handle anything that is thrown at you – good and bad – as you learn to build your skills and learn what you're naturally good at.

Mainly Cs:

You lack confidence in your abilities.

You are rather nervous or too modest in nature, and sometimes this leads you to belittle yourself. Many people appreciate modesty, especially among the great and the good of this world. It might be a good idea to take a step back to consider what you've accomplished in life and the talents you possess in order to compare yourself to others who seem so sure of themselves. You may be pleasantly surprised when you look back on your career path and be more prone to believe in your own abilities in the future. If fear of taking the lead, especially in the company of other people, is causing your lack of self-confidence, try to mingle more with others. Play your strengths. If, for example, you are good at chess, join a club. If you like foreign languages, sign up for a course. The more your confidence grows, the more others will be encouraged to trust you and the more you will succeed.

CHAPTER 2

WHY DO YOU WANT CONFIDENCE – AND WHY DO YOU NEED IT?

These might be obvious questions to you. You want confidence because having no confidence makes you miserable. You need confidence because having no confidence is stopping you from moving forward in your life. We hope that the above questions are already making you think about the difference between want and need. We're not trying to scramble your brain with philosophical discussions. If anything, we want to simplify how you view confidence so that it doesn't appear unattainable.

Confidence is one of those words that's bandied about all over the place, yet it means different things to different people. In Chapter 1 we went deep into the definitions. In this chapter we're moving towards helping you tune your definition of what's real confidence to the real you.

You may be at a stage of looking at people around you, almost like browsing online for things you want to buy. You need a laptop so you look online, you think about cost, maybe you Google best laptops for £x and you read the reviews until you decide what you want. You only need a laptop to use at home, mostly you use your phone and tablet, and you don't want to spend much. It can still be a minefield deciding which one to pick, right? But when you look at your life and then look at confident people who have what you want in life, are you doing as much analysis about what you want and need?

In our consumer society we spend a lot of time considering our spending, from mobile phone providers to holiday deals. We need to apply the same thinking to our inner lives. That's why you've bought this book of course, but we're not just going to give you a formula, let you try it out and then move on because it doesn't suit you. Our approach isn't one size fits all.

Asking yourself why you want confidence and why you need confidence will help you clarify the way forward. Pursuing confidence is a relatively new phenomenon in our society, which is in itself interesting. The late Psychiatrist Dr Wayne Dyer's best-selling *Your Erroneous Zones* (Little Brown), for example, came out in 1976. The index does not include confidence. There's so much preoccupation with confidence now that it can cloud what you really want (your dreams) and what you need (to thrive and be happy in life).

LOW CONFIDENCE IS A GREAT STARTING POINT

" Confidence is about how smart you think you are. "

Dr Tomas Chamorro-Premuzic, Psychologist and Professor of Business Psychology at UCL

Tomas Chamorro-Premuzic likens confidence to a powerful image of an inner thermostat that senses how likely we are to reach the level of performance we desire. His take on confidence is reassuring: namely that we don't need as much as we think we do. Becoming competent is what we need to focus on. But maybe it's all very well for a confident person to say this. After all, what use is competence *without* confidence? Chamorro-Premuzic is inspiring in his insistence that under-confidence plus high competence leads to exceptional performance. He doesn't deny that, yes, confidence would also make you feel good about yourself; however, it's the only advantage he identifies.

Well isn't that a pretty huge advantage? Isn't feeling good something we need? Well it might be. Only that's a separate issue. If you think you *need* confidence because you *want* tangible success, what this prolific academic and personality assessment expert is saying is that accomplishments need not be related to confidence. And if you don't feel good becoming competent and successful, your continuing lack of confidence is still a good thing. You'll just go on to achieve more. In other words, as neatly put by Chamorro-Premuzic: 'Under confident people who are competent tend to medicate their insecurities with accomplishments.'

If you had to reread that a couple of times because it sent a shockwave through your brain, yes, what this business psychologist is saying is that lack of confidence is a motivational force that can result in high achievements. It might be hard to absorb what Chamorro-Premuzic is saying from a non-confident standpoint, but at least knowing that low confidence isn't a bad starting point can help you move forward. Diverting your attention to becoming more competent is a lot easier and more tangible than wrestling with abstract confidence.

66 There is absolutely no point in having confidence while being incompetent. 99

Dr Tomas Chamorro-Premuzic, Psychologist and Professor of Business Psychology at UCL

DR TOMAS CHAMORRO-PREMUZIC ON HAPPINESS AND DISSATISFACTION

'Ignorance is bliss, at least in the short-run. If 30 fewer IQ points would increase happiness, would you take the offer? I wouldn't because you would miss out on the complexities of life and your contribution to society would be smaller. Our notion of happiness is unfortunately dependent on feeling good. In reality we should be happy when we are doing good. Happiness is a modern narcissistic concept. We did not evolve to this stage of civilization because of happiness; in fact, dissatisfaction is the mother of progress. If we were really truly happy, we would cease to evolve.'

IDENTIFY WHAT YOU WANT

You may have come to believe that what you want and need is one big confidence implant into your brain. It's all too easy to fall back on confidence as the missing link for anything that's not going well in your life. You've moved to a new area and think you need confidence to make new friends. You've finally found a job after a long spell of unemployment but feel intimidated because you have no confidence in technology and you feel like an idiot. You want to have a baby but there's no partner in sight, and you just don't have the confidence to meet someone through online dating. You'd really like to be in a steady relationship but you're not confident about being intimate with someone.

By focusing on exactly what you want, you can in fact figure out what you need. To take the above example, this might be anything from:

- Information – what can you do that will maximize your opportunities to meet like-minded people?
- Skills – what do you need to learn, what knowledge are you lacking?
- Advice – what's the best way to go about dating, what would suit your personality most?

The more specific you are, the more you can focus on what it is you need to master. Think of it as the difference between not knowing how many people you have to cook for and what their dietary issues are, and knowing that you have to cook for six people including one dairy-intolerant carnivore, one vegetarian and one vegan. It's the difference between not knowing where to start and taking a risk that could go wrong (a meat-based BBQ for 16 people), or planning (a Greek meze-style buffet with something for everyone).

When we identify something we want, we are able to work with our natural, human psychological needs. In Chapter 1 we identified self-efficacy as an important basis for the definition of confidence. Because self-efficacy is one of our three basic psychological needs (along with being autonomous and being able to relate to others) we can learn to find confidence by pinpointing what we want. As Dr Ilona Boniwell explains, this goes back to when we learnt to walk. As toddlers we master how to take steps without falling down until we manage to walk.

> **"As human beings we have a basic *need* to master situations. Our confidence comes from mastering our environment."**
>
> Dr Ilona Boniwell, positive psychologist

If you think of going through life as a series of different challenges to master, you will begin to break down the barrier of no confidence. It might be that people have told you that you have no confidence or that all you need is confidence. However, it's important to remember that people say things for the sake of saying something without necessarily knowing what they are talking about. Sometimes they do so because they think this is supportive and helpful, or because on a conscious or unconscious level, reminding you that you lack confidence makes them feel better. Some people like to talk without thinking because it makes them feel good and not talking brings up their insecurities and makes them feel bad.

The key here is not to give others material. Building real confidence does involve going within and doing some soul searching as well as doing some solid research into what you need (including advice, skills, knowledge, information, experts, networking opportunities, and even new supportive like-minded friends). If what you need to master is writing your family's incredible history, but you are daunted by the prospect of writing, then focusing on confidence is pretty much a waste of time. It's not confidence that will get you writing, it's starting to research and compile your information; it's taking an introductory course on writing, followed by a weekly course, joining a writers' group, and allocating time to spend every week on your project. As your family memoir begins to shape you will organically become confident.

Of course, your lack of confidence may be so chronic that you feel at a loss. Perhaps you have no idea what you want. Even if we waved a magic wand and bestowed confidence on you, you still wouldn't know what you want – and the confidence wouldn't be real. If you focus your attention on discovering what it is you want, then your attention won't be hijacked by a desire for something abstract.

WORK ON YOURSELF

The big question of what you want can be overwhelming, and of course we don't want you to be so overwhelmed that you give up on confidence (a natural reaction). Here's where we'll let you in on how confident people approach the big questions. Confident people know what they are confident in because that's where their knowledge, expertise, experience, and passion lie. Confident people who are genuinely confident are self-aware and can pinpoint gaps in their knowledge or skills. When they need to develop areas in which they have these gaps they work on themselves, gaining the necessary skills, knowledge, and experience.

When voice and leadership coach Patsy Rodenburg isn't running the Voice department at the Guildhall School of Music and Drama or coaching the world's leading theatre stars, she coaches leaders and athletes. Stars, leaders and athletes might all appear to be confident, particularly to someone who feels frustrated and blocked. But try flipping that last assumption and reframing it to: stars, leaders and athletes who are top of their fields continue to work on themselves to develop confidence in new areas.

Part of the complexity around confidence is how it fluctuates in different areas of our lives. If you feel you have no confidence in any area of your life, or you find it hard to be specific about what you want, you can start by using Rodenburg's four categories of confidence: physical, intellectual, emotional and spiritual.

Start by asking yourself which of these areas is currently most important to you, or what you would like from each area. So, for example, you might realize that your key interest is in spirituality and the knowledge you've gained through reading and going to workshops has made you realize you are unfulfilled emotionally and intellectually. Let's say your interest in spirituality has led you to regular classes in Tai Chi and your body and mind have benefited. In turn, you realize that physically you do have confidence. You know you need to identify more specifics for the intellectual and emotional areas of your life. As you ask yourself questions, you'll begin to see the answers. Is your job not stimulating enough (so you need a new job)? Have you been on your own too much (so you need to find the courage to be in a relationship again)?

“It all goes back to knowledge.”

Patsy Rodenburg, OBE, voice and leadership coach

By breaking down your life and analysing it, you may come up with some simple solutions to your lack of confidence. Rodenburg works with Olympians, who as top athletes tend to of course be confident physically. They have also mastered the art of presence, which is why they have won medals. But they turn to Rodenburg when they need to make speeches because this is an entirely new area for them. They are masters at working with their bodies and mastering their bodies, but they are not used to working in an intellectual way. So they have to work at this.

IS IT LACK OR LOSS OF CONFIDENCE?

Even if on the surface you were confident in the past, you may be facing up to the fact that inside you've always been deeply insecure. Lack of confidence means you sense it was always missing. Or this might not be the case at all. Perhaps loss of confidence is more accurate for you. You may have been successful, happy, and with that, confident, but events and circumstances have zapped your confidence or slowly chipped away at it. Working out what has happened to you can help you approach why you want and need confidence. For somebody who has been able to fake confidence whilst leading a successful life on the surface, it might be more important to find inner confidence that matches what's on the outside so as not to feel fake. At the other end of the scale, someone who has experienced confidence in the past may be yearning to get back to feeling good and on top.

Both lack and loss of confidence can manifest in different ways. For many people, part of admiring confident people is envying their ability to take risks in their stride rather than get caught up in procrastination. Yet risk is by no means confidence. Reckless decisions can be based on fear masquerading as confidence and that can be due to lack of real confidence or loss of confidence.

66Risk is confidence when informed and thought through.99

Annie Ashdown, confidence coach

Of course, life isn't so straightforward and you may realize that you're a mixture of both. You may have lost your confidence professionally because the recession wiped out your work and your identity was based on your work. Add to this the fact that perhaps you've never really, truthfully felt confident socially. Maybe when you were younger you could wing it because everyone went to the pub and you could cover up your inhibitions by drinking. It's not unusual for people to find themselves losing their confidence because of a life event, and this loss makes them aware that confidence in another area was never too strong.

The most reassuring thing we can say to you is that neither state is insurmountable. One of the reasons there is some outstanding advice and help out there is because people who have experienced lack and loss of confidence have bounced back to help others gain confidence. Confidence coach Annie Ashdown is herself a good case study of somebody who personified confidence. As a child actress, then a model, followed by working in TV and being an entrepreneur, on the surface she had success, money, status. But she also suffered from eating disorders, terrible relationships and bullying. 'I didn't have the inner confidence to sustain the success,' she admits, 'I simply didn't feel worthy.' Overcoming her problems gave her the impetus to train to help others. When she started coaching people she quickly discovered many celebrities and household business names shared her former experience of 'the imposter syndrome', appearing confident but lacking real confidence.

EMBRACE CULTURE

Feeding the mind with great culture is one of the easiest ways to change the way you feel about yourself. As Patsy Rodenburg reminds us 'we learn through great storytelling'. Instead of worrying about confidence, find confident role models in theatre or classic literature. And for a different twist on a book group,

why not discuss what confidence means in relation to the characters in modern fiction? The classics have become classics because they are stories that have resonated with audiences since they were originally created. By analysing characters other than yourself, you give your mind a rest and experience a fictional character's journey that may be similar to yours.

People are able to kid themselves for a while at least that they are confident because a natural aptitude can lead to success, whether that's a talent for singing or a knack for making money. What's happening here, as Ashdown explains, is the ego is driving the part with the amazing talent, and it's driving really well. But if you still feel inadequate in other areas of your life, sooner or later there's no hiding from that lack of confidence. Sooner or later not only does it emerge, but it takes over and derails the ego driving the part of you that has the natural talent or aptitude.

66 If we don't have confidence, we leave ourselves wide open and vulnerable to disrespect, and to emotional and even physical abuse. Living in this fast-paced, challenging world with low confidence is dangerous. 99

Annie Ashdown, confidence coach

The big message here is that if confidence isn't real it's not enough to sustain us through life. We need real confidence to back up what we're doing outwardly; otherwise we can get ill, be prone to addictions, and can be very unhappy.

If external circumstances have eroded your confidence you may feel worn out if not burnt out. You may have lapsed into asking how anyone can cultivate confidence when they can't control what happens to them. The fact that you're reading this shows that something inside you refuses to give up. If external circumstances are responsible for you losing your confidence, it may not be confidence that you need but something else, like a total change or time to recover. As you'll see from the following story about life coach Dawn Breslin, success is not immune to biology or the economy. Many of Breslin's clients now have had similar experiences to hers. They *need* to get back to who they are, but aren't sure how to take that step to regain their confidence.

DAWN BRESLIN ON HANDLING HER LOSS OF CONFIDENCE

'Twenty years ago I was a high-flying advertising sales exec, living in a big mansion house with a husband and lots of money in the bank and everything was fantastic. Then I had my baby daughter and for nine months she wouldn't stop crying. In that period I went from being a confident, self-assured, bubbly gregarious individual to believing I was a useless mother and wife, that I was fat, unattractive and unemployable. Like so many others, when we go through challenging life changes, we can easily lose our self-belief. I lost my foundation completely. This stuff creeps up on you as negative, destructive thinking creeps in. It's so gradual. One day you're on top of the world and then a subtle erosion kicks in, you lose your confidence over time.

Listening to an aunt's advice and going to a Louise L Hay workshop was my wake-up call for the work I do now. I wondered how many other people felt like this. So I trained with Louise L Hay, Bernie Segal and in NLP (neurolinguistic programming). I had a fire in my belly and I wanted to get my message out there into the media. I wanted to be on GMTV talking about something meaningful. I was petrified, I'd never spoken to a group in my life, but slowly and gradually I overcome my fears.

Around five years ago I lost the business opportunity of a lifetime when a deal with a multinational fell through because of the recession.

I spent two years trying to run the project by myself which resulted in me having a mini-breakdown. I was £100,000 in debt, my relationship ended, and I was burnt out. I thought I'd never work again and my reputation was flushed down the toilet. Probably no one even noticed. That was simply my ego having a meltdown. I had to take the time to repair my confidence and energy and get back to me, and that process took two years.'

We saw in Chapter 1 that making assumptions about other people being confident is unwise because this might not be accurate. In this chapter we've guided you to analyse confidence in relation to you in terms of what you want and need. You might want to gain confidence in business presentations because you need to pitch to financial partners to back your business idea. One of the biggest revelations we hope you'll take from this chapter and this book is that low confidence can be a good thing as it can spur you on to become successful because your focus will be on developing skills and becoming competent. By identifying what you want and need you can help yourself pinpoint specific areas in your life so that instead of looking for a confidence brolly to pull out, you develop confidence skills to take you through any storm. Instead of wishful thinking combined with negative self-beliefs, we hope you will start taking action to become competent in any area you decide to focus on.

Distinguishing between lack or loss of confidence, or a combination, can give you greater understanding of what you need. If you need to take time out or work on something else before you tackle confidence, that process in itself will give you confidence. If your confidence has been eroded after a terrible year, what you need first is time to recuperate and time to think about what you want.

ASK YOURSELF

Q I want confidence to ....?

Q I need confidence to ....?

Q What frustrates me is..............?

Q What gets in the way of me doing what I really want do is my ....?

Q Every day I would like to ....?

FOCUS ON FEELINGS INSTEAD OF GOALS

Most advice on improving our lives is based on identifying goals and working towards these. But if your baseline is lack of confidence, setting goals won't help you develop the confidence to achieve these. So for the moment, put aside the goals and what you want to achieve and approach yourself from an entirely different perspective: how you want to feel.

Dawn Breslin suggests finding *how* you want to feel in your life by creating a feelings collage. Take some time to yourself with your favourite magazines and weekend supplements. Tear out images and words and phrases that capture your ideal feelings. 'Get away from looking for pictures of ideal homes and jobs and anything material,' says Breslin. 'You might find someone relaxing on a hammock and the words *rejuvenate, inspire*. Use your feelings board to identify five feelings you'd like to experience every day.'

ARE YOU OVER-CONFIDENT OR UNDER-CONFIDENT?

Real confidence is about self-awareness and knowing yourself well enough to know where your strengths lie, where you need to develop yourself and where there are gaps in your knowledge, skills and experience. Confidence is not about trying to pretend you know more than you do or 'faking it 'til you make it'. Real confidence is about going within and doing some soul searching as well as doing some solid research in what you need (training, practice, a mentor?) to help get you where you want to be. Confidence comes by becoming genuinely good at something, and building on natural skills and talents. Complete this test and discover if you're under-confident or over-confident:

Test by: Hélène Vecchiali
Translated by Nora Mahony

QUESTION 1

Describing your professional skills, you would say:

A. I always figure it out in the end.
B. I'm underemployed.
C. I could use more training.
D. I'm comfortable in my role and have opportunities to move forward.

QUESTION 2

Arriving at a party where you know no-one, you think:

A. No one's paying attention to me.
B. What can I do to get noticed?
C. Why is everyone looking at me?
D. I'll see if I'm in the mood to talk to anyone.

QUESTION 3

Your personal life at the moment makes you feel:

A. Confident in your pulling power.
B. Like Don Juan, but sexier.
C. Like you need some love.
D. Zen and radiant.

QUESTION 4

When you get through a task singlehandedly, you:

A. Shout it from the rooftops.
B. Make sure the boss knows.
C. Feel quietly pleased with yourself.
D. Build on your success.

QUESTION 5

When a colleague has a good idea, you:

A. Let him know that without you, it wouldn't have been possible.

B. Say nothing; it's his job to have good ideas.

C. Shower him with compliments.

D. Congratulate him and appreciate his contribution.

QUESTION 6

In your opinion, a good boss must be:

A. Affable and winning.

B. Ambitious and shrewd.

C. Discreet and reserved.

D. Competent and fair.

QUESTION 7

Before responding to a job offer or going to an interview, you:

A. Go without giving it a second thought; you'll know soon enough.

B. See what strings you can pull.

C. Practise your presentation several times in front of friends.

D. Research the business, its directors, and the position in question.

QUESTION 8

You're redoing your CV. You:

A. Beef up your education levels and key experiences.

B. Inflate your job descriptions in places.

C. Forget to include details that could really help you.

D. Check there aren't any typos.

QUESTION 9

When you look in a mirror, you think:

A. Stunning, with a smile to put Hollywood in its place.
B. Good; no more, no less.
C. Not bad, could do better.
D. Not bad at all.

QUESTION 10

You want to get promoted at work. You:

A. Talk yourself up everywhere and anywhere.
B. Invite the HR director to dinner.
C. Wonder if it's really the right time.
D. Apply for on-the-job training.

QUESTION 11

You haven't heard from a very close friend in two weeks. You:

A. Tell yourself that clearly, they don't deserve you.
B. Get a mutual friend to make sure they call you.
C. Think that they must be angry at you.
D. Call to see how it's going.

QUESTION 12

At a final interview, a 'hole' in your CV comes up that corresponds to two years of unemployment. You respond:

A. 'Those two years allowed me to dig deep and come back twice as strong.'
B. 'I took two years' sabbatical to get some perspective.'
C. With nothing. You lower your gaze and stay quiet.
D. 'Those two years were difficult, but they allowed me to take stock of my strengths and weaknesses.'

Mostly As

You're overselling yourself.

You often feel that you are not good enough so you make up for it by making yourself the centre of attention.

You're afraid of being exposed and often worry: Am I the right person for the job? Do I know enough? Consider your need to inflate your own importance. Try to stop overcompensating – it doesn't do you any good, and at times can make you look like a fraud. Being yourself will usually be enough to show how valuable you are. Try it in a low-stakes situation and you might be surprised by your success.

Mostly Bs

You're blagging too much.

You're a charmer, with plenty of good qualities, but you're an expert in hot air, pulling the wool over people's eyes and even playing the odd trick. You like to make life easy for yourself.

The only catch is that you don't really feel at home in your own skin. You worry that people might see through you. What if you decided to put all that energy into developing a more honest approach to life? Work on it, ask for help when you need it, and you'll see that it's infinitely less exhausting to be yourself than to try to be one step ahead of everyone else all the time.

Mostly Cs

You doubt yourself too much.

You are a champion of undervaluing yourself. Avoid situations that stress you out by first making peace with yourself. Your friends, books or time with a therapist can all help. Talk about it, think about the path you've taken, and occasionally take a fresh look at your skills. You need to work on the things that bring you joy, your beliefs, desires, your love life and your fears. Be realistic, and try to be a little kinder to yourself!

Mostly Ds

You are self-aware.

You're aware of your talents, strengths and weaknesses, and you feel at peace with both yourself and others. You know how to listen and you express yourself with diplomacy and fairness. You know how to make your experiences – good and bad – work for you to improve your relationships and develop your professional skills.

With your skills, it would be a waste not to develop them further. Talent must be grown, or it withers and dies. Another trap is taking too much of a back seat. Learn to be curious, and keep surprising yourself and others.

CHAPTER 3

HOW DOES REAL CONFIDENCE FEEL? BEING COMFORTABLE IN YOUR OWN SKIN

Now there's a question that can often turn into wishful thinking. What would it feel like to be Amal or George Clooney? Would we stride out to work every day with not a scrap of doubt about what we're wearing and with that look of meaning professional business? Would we be totally cool about paparazzi trailing us?

What we really need to ask is how does true confidence feel *to me*? In fact we need to phrase that slightly differently: how does confidence feel when I really am me? How do I know I am the real me?

COMING FROM THE HEART

Let's take A-list voice and leadership coach Patsy Rodenburg's analogy of the three circles of energy. The first circle is inward and introspective. The third is outward, seeking attention. This is the jolly, enthusiastic, loud, brash confidence that Rodenburg says is in fact bluff. In the second circle, energy flows in two directions: inwards and outwards. Now that might initially sound like a difficult idea to grasp when you're thinking 'yes, but what does this mean to me?' and you need a sense of how you're going to experience confidence. Rodenburg says that all great performers, athletes and leaders are examples of second circle energy, giving and receiving, being fully present *with* themselves *and* others. And it's this duality that she says is confidence.

In any situation where you're lacking in confidence, you'll be focused predominantly on you, so you're likely to be in the first circle of energy. Let's say you're making a presentation at work. Your thought process might be something like: 'I'm rubbish, I'm making a mess of this, I'm boring, no one is listening, I can't get my words out.' You might be so focused on feeling negative towards yourself that by not focusing on the group of people listening to you, you could be missing vital signs. Maybe some of them are smiling; maybe some are concentrating hard on what you have to say. By just making a simple switch from worrying about yourself to observing yourself and others you will experience being with yourself and with other people in a different way.

Rodenburg encourages us to be present with others and to give generously, both when we speak and when we listen. By reminding yourself to do this, you'll find you feel more alive and, without realizing it, you'll have prompted yourself to be in a more confident state of mind.

" If you can listen to someone, you have a confidence which has humanity rather than imposed confidence. Coming forward and being open takes courage – that's confidence. "

Patsy Rodenburg, OBE, voice and leadership coach

KNOWING YOU ARE DOING THE RIGHT THING

One of the biggest problems with lack of confidence is doubting yourself in every way, from what you say to any decisions you take. You may have come across other advice that advocates not worrying about these feelings because the confidence will follow. Only it doesn't, does it? That's not because there's anything wrong with you. If confidence is real then you will feel good about your decisions and actions. You'll want to have a go at whatever it is, you'll have a sense that if you don't move home or change career or turn your hobby into a business you'll never know. When confidence is real, it's not that we feel sure, we feel we *want* to see what happens.

BE MORE OF YOURSELF

Whatever you naturally are – whether it's funny, supportive, nurturing, opinionated, passionate, or something else – don't shut this down completely at work. Adjust the volume on this quality so that it's still there even if are not revealing it to the max. For example, if you hate your job and feel there's nothing that inspires passion, can you bring your passion to work in any way? Perhaps you can run at lunchtime, or bring cakes, or set up a lunchtime book group. Finding ways to retain your core identity boosts your confidence immediately.

Life coach Dawn Breslin always tries to get across to clients making changes in their lives (particularly after challenging life events that have wiped out their confidence) that major changes are a process of growth. If we're following our heart (in other words following a little calling inside us) this will feel exciting rather than terrifying. It's a nervy excitement because you're doing something you've never done before, but this feeling is entirely normal and natural.

> **" Feeling good in your skin means you can walk forward knowing who you are and what you believe in. Confidence is really knowing you are doing the right thing. "**
>
> Dawn Breslin, confidence coach

You probably feel that whatever the definition of confidence, it doesn't feel bad, which means it must involve feeling good. But there's a danger here in attaching this 'feeling good' to other things, in particular success. Here we want to clarify that feeling good about yourself in terms of confidence is not about feeling happy or achieving your goals. Real confidence doesn't disappear when things don't go right.

Having been through major life traumas that include homelessness and losing a partner to suicide, as well as having been enormously successful in her former careers, confidence coach Annie Ashdown cautions us about associating confidence with success, particularly as success can be down to luck. Let's say you win the lottery, or inherit money, will this give you real confidence? You may feel euphoric for a while, but no, luck doesn't give you confidence. When you develop real confidence this becomes part of being resilient during tough times.

"Inner confidence means feeling good about yourself even when things are going horribly wrong. "

Annie Ashdown, confidence coach

RELAXED, CALM AND A LITTLE EXCITED

Definitions and discussions are all very well, but can we *feel* confidence in our mind and body and, if so, what exactly are the components of that feeling? When was the last time someone gave you an accurate description of the inner experience of a particular feeling? We don't just want to give you vague information and leave you hanging, we want to be as precise as possible. And what can be more precise than science and what is going on physiologically in the body?

DR NITASHA BULDEO ON THE PHYSIOLOGICAL STATE OF CONFIDENCE

'We all have a state when we are relaxed, excited and happy. We know how that feels. It's that relaxed anticipation. And that's exactly how confidence feels: I am relaxed, I know I can do this, I'm excited. Confidence is about the internal state. It's introspective plus it's how your body feels. Your pulse rate will be within your normal range, and within your relaxed state. And you feel that slight twinge in your gut. It's like you are anticipating something exciting is going to happen; you're going to do your thing and you feel wonderful, nothing throws you off balance.

The internal state changes when we're not feeling confident. The heart rate increases, there may be increased bowel movements or upset tummies. The feeling is not being on top of things.

Authentic confidence is based on knowing what we know, knowing what we are capable of doing, and that means we can admit what we don't know and take time to master this. If we're prepared we feel we can handle anything thrown our way. It's not luck.

Sports people can control their heart rate and respiratory rate by giving the brain and muscles the oxygen they need to work efficiently. If you develop internal body awareness, you know the state your body needs to be in to thrive so you never get stuck.'

We hope we've given you a precise sense of exactly how real confidence feels from within and that this inspires you to be yourself. Being comfortable in your own skin means going within but not staying within. Developing an awareness of yourself in relation to others and how others relate to you is not complicated. It's about being human, being the best we can be. But that doesn't mean pushing yourself or being hard on yourself. It may be that a particular situation has drained you of confidence and in order to get to the real you, you need some time to rest and re-energize. Far from being a sign of weakness, this is a sign that you value yourself.

If you can reconnect with how you feel when things are going well and you are happy, this will remind you that confidence is within you. Even if you're going through a terrible time and feel you can't remember the last time you felt happy or excited, there will be happy periods or happy moments that you can think back to and identify, even if it is just buying an ice cream. Knowing that you have experienced a state that feels like confidence will give you courage.

ASK YOURSELF

Q When did you feel last confident doing something? How did that feel?

Q Think of a time when you pretended to be confident. How did that feel?

Q When you go into a situation lacking in confidence, what is happening in your body?

Q What is happening in your body when you are calm? And excited?

HOW COMFORTABLE ARE YOU IN YOUR OWN SKIN?

If real confidence is about being authentic and being comfortable in your own skin – do you know how that feels? How do you express your emotions – both the negative and positive? How comfortable do you feel about being honest about your feelings? What does it mean to you to be true to yourself? If confidence is based on knowing what we know, and what we're capable of doing, how does it feel then to sometimes admit you don't know what you're doing? How can you be comfortable in your own skin – when things aren't going well? Take this test to discover how comfortable you feel being authentically you – warts and all.

Test by Christophe André
Translated by Nora Mahony

QUESTION 1

Telling the truth is:

A. Healthy. There's nothing worse than hypocrisy. (1 point)
B. Desirable. But not all the time. (2 points)
C. Risky. You should always think about it first. (3 points)
D. Pointless, dangerous and misleading. There are so many possible truths… (4 points)

QUESTION 2

You realize that someone is lying to you. You:

A. Act like nothing has happened. (4 points)
B. Tell them right away so that they can explain. (1 point)
C. Let them know that you know, discreetly; why catch someone out or make them angry? (2 points)
D. Will talk to them about it, but not for a long time. (3 points)

QUESTION 3

How much do you talk about your private life?

A. Never. My business is my business. (4 points)
B. Often enough. But only if it comes up in conversation. (2 points)
C. All the time. Everyone likes to talk about themselves – it's the only thing worth talking about. (1 point)
D. Occasionally. I'd discuss my life with my closest friends. (3 points)

QUESTION 4

For you, following fashion is:

A. Easier, so that you can be like everyone else. (2 points)
B. Fun. It's a way to express your personality. (1 point)
C. Superficial… but you have to keep up with the times. (3 points)
D. Meh. Timeless pieces are the way to go. (4 points)

QUESTION 5

In your relationships with others:

A. People would say that you're reserved. (3 points)

B. You hurt, annoy and astound people. You certainly make an impression. (1 point)

C. You tend to be well liked. (2 points)

D. You have a reputation for being reserved, even self-effacing. (4 points)

QUESTION 6

On giving your opinion:

A. Someone would have to insist if they wanted to find out what you thought. (4 points)

B. You wait to be asked before giving your opinion. (3 points)

C. You always offer your point of view, but it's never in the form of an order. (2 points)

D. You give your opinion even without being asked for it. (1 point)

QUESTION 7

At a business party, your nose starts to itch:

A. You scratch it without even thinking about it. What's the problem? (1 point)

B. You brush the end of your nose discreetly with your fingertip. (2 points)

C. You leave for a moment to scratch it properly. (3 points)

D. You'd rather soldier on for the rest of the party. (4 points)

QUESTION 8

Do you keep a diary?

A. I'd rather live my life than write about it, you know? (1 point)

B. I think about it often, but I never actually do. (2 points)

C. I've started and stopped a few times. (3 points)

D. Of course, I love it. (4 points)

QUESTION 9

You've been invited to a boring party. You:

A. Dream up an excuse so you don't have to go. (3 points)
B. Send your apologies diplomatically. (2 points)
C. Answer, 'No thanks, that's just not my kind of thing.' (1 point)
D. Go, reluctantly, but leave early. (4 points)

QUESTION 10

You want to break up with someone after a month:

A. You send them a text. (3 points)
B. You avoid them and hope they get the message. (4 points)
C. You arrange to meet them for coffee and tell them everything. (1 point)
D. You write them a long letter that explains all your feelings and post it. (2 points)

10–18 points

Unfiltered: just you

Truth and sincerity are your core values. You know full well that the truth can hurt and upset people, but you believe that in the long run, nothing can beat it. You're adept at telling the 'real truth': your truths, which can be challenging.

There are downsides: people have to take you as you are. You're not always mindful of others, at least not initially. It can come across as insensitive, and you can offend and anger people, which takes time and diplomacy to fix. Consider taking it down a notch.

19–25 points

Authentic: a managed you

Your motto is: 'Being myself without causing any drama.' You know how to moderate your behaviour and choose your words in keeping with your company and surroundings. You think of others before you act, and before you speak. A supporter of the 'managed truth', you are able to put just about anything into words, but gently and appropriately.

26–31 points

Reserved: a curated you

You would only ever tell the truth – no question of lying – but perhaps not the whole truth as you wouldn't want to hurt anyone's feelings. Good manners and rules of conduct are important to you. Your reserved take on how to relate to other people and your self-control aren't supposed to close people out, but are a considered way of letting them in. It isn't a sign of distrust; it's prudence.

32–40 points

Hidden: a silenced you

Authenticity is just an illusion to you: we have dozens of facets, and we change throughout our lives. Being true to ourselves is also risky: what does it achieve to hurt people, to impose ourselves on others, to expose our true selves to others in the first place? You don't tell the truth if it's toxic. Besides, who can claim to be telling the truth? What we think today we might not think tomorrow. You don't act on principle but by pragmatism. You observe for a long time before you act, and think long and hard before you speak. Keeping this up as habit can lead to problems: you almost never let go, you hide your feelings, you think too much about what others think. To show any kind of great wisdom, you'll have to reveal your true self, at least with people you trust.

2 WHY DO YOU LACK CONFIDENCE?

CHAPTER 4

WHERE DOES YOUR LACK OF CONFIDENCE COME FROM?

W here does a lack of confidence come from? Take a wild guess. It might be a definite 'childhood' for anyone who feels they got knocked back by parents and teachers. For others it may be a reserved 'childhood' if parents did their best but teachers were critical (or vice versa). For those who are baffled because their childhood was pretty 'normal' or they're confident in some areas and not in others, the answer might be 'childhood?' with a question mark.

Here's where you need to remember that defining confidence is complex in itself. If you're caught up in 'I've made such a mess of my life', this lack of confidence could be the result of life circumstances. Add divorce + redundancy + bereavement = feeling a failure. Feeling a failure will inevitably affect confidence.

One way or another our earliest experiences shape us. It's *how* that can be surprising. Let's take a 2015 study at the University at Buffalo[1] which showed that people from a negative background who have low self-esteem have higher self-clarity than adults who manage to overcome their difficult backgrounds and achieve high self-esteem.

Psychologists define self-clarity as our ability to confidently describe ourselves. Previous studies have indicated that the better we feel about ourselves, the clearer we are about *who* we are. The Buffalo study, however, was the first to look at the influence of early family experiences. People with low self-esteem have lower expectations, but this means they have higher self-clarity because without high self-esteem they're not disappointed when things go wrong. Until there are more studies we can't draw definite conclusions, but it's interesting to bear in mind that however bad we feel about ourselves this isn't necessarily a bad thing.

When we talk about 'roots' we tend to think of a tree. But in the case of confidence maybe what we need to think about is a garden. Some of our plants do really well and are blooming. Others die off fast. Some never even develop roots from the seeds. Viewed this way something else becomes apparent: a garden may be healthy and gorgeous and then be destroyed by a storm; a vegetable patch may never quite get growing because of the slugs; a fox may rampage over beautiful flowers; baby pine trees may have to be moved a couple of times until their right position is found. And of course, we have to look after the garden.

IS CONFIDENCE IN YOUR GENES OR YOUR ENVIRONMENT?

Part of our psychological profile is biological and genetic. The figure most quoted by psychologists is a staggering 50 per cent. A major 2009 study by Professor Robert Plomin and Corina Greven at the Institute of Psychiatry[2] King's College, London, concluded that self-confidence is genetic and can predict a child's achievement at school. The study looked at identical twins (with the same genes) and non-identical twins (same environment).

On one level an influential study like this suggests that as some people are naturally confident, those who don't have the genetic advantage are at a disadvantage. However, this 50 per cent biology that we arrive with is affected by our environment, namely parents and family, where we live, and school. So even without self-confidence genes, there can be something else in our genetic make-up that helps us develop confidence. There are all sorts of traits you might have inherited that contribute to developing your confidence. Let's say you've been a bookworm from the moment you could read and thrive at absorbing lots of information. Or you've been able to pick up languages before you could even write. These are natural aptitudes that you can use as a foundation for developing confidence.

Added to your biological/genetic make-up are your childhood experiences. This fusion is like the programming for your inner software. There might be glitches that go back to childhood. Some people are baffled as to why they have problems as adults despite a happy childhood, whilst others wonder why they can't get over and past their unhappy early years. There's no easy explanation to this, it's the complexity and wonder of the human psyche. Our brains are wired up to remember everything in some way.

Think of this as our inner computer software, what's known as the limbic system. Just as your computer freezes or plays up or does odd things with no 'rational' explanation, your brain does exactly the same. Something now triggers something from the past, but this is unconscious. This is the reason we respond to anything from soap operas to theatre, pop songs to opera. The ancient Greeks developed drama because it was a release for stored emotion.

And this is why for no apparent reason, from one moment to another you might go from confident to wobbly. Let's say you're having a good day and you see a parking attendant approaching your car. You know full well you're early and you won't get a parking ticket. But the sight of the attendant triggers something in you, you can feel your heart beating faster and you get agitated and nervous. Who knows what has triggered this. You don't need to worry about it saying something about your level of confidence, because it's normal. As acting coach and psychologist Niki Flacks says: 'This nonsense lives in all of us.'

"We are all in our most primitive selves ruled by fears."

Niki Flacks, acting coach, psychologist, therapist

DR ILONA BONIWELL ON HOW WE RESPOND TO POSITIVE AND NEGATIVE INFLUENCES

'Some people are genetically prone to negative and positive influences. This is good news because it means that these children can go further if their parents encourage them in a positive way.

When you receive mainly negative feedback as a child, this doesn't help your confidence develop. This is because nobody is validating your successful accomplishment of tasks, so you *don't have the feeling of accomplishment – so you don't develop confidence.*

But validation for unsuccessful tasks or no effort becomes useless. Validation for just anything leads to low self-esteem because the child knows deep down what they're doing is not good. Modern positive parenting is as negative as negative parenting. This goes back to [Stanford University] psychologist Carol Dweck's theory of mindset, which was developed over several decades of research. There are two types of mindset: fixed or growth. With a growth mindset we believe our mind can grow. If we give a child feedback like "you are a great genius", what we are confirming is a fixed mindset, so a child internalizes that they are clever. When they then hit an obstacle that gives them the feedback that they are not clever, they can't manage. Their reaction is to disengage. This unmerited positive praise can have the negative function of building a fixed mindset which is unprepared for difficulties in life: there is nothing I can do, so I won't do it. So your confidence suffers as much as it would have from negative parenting.

Although there are no scientific studies to confirm this, parents probably have more influence than school because if things aren't going well at school parents can talk you through things, help you with homework or point out you didn't prepare enough. And as a child you realize there are many teachers and they are different, whereas even if your parents divorce, your mum and dad are the same.

Children get more confident the happier they are. Confidence can be undone in adolescence, but it can also be rebuilt. Positive adolescence is about children acquiring as many experiences as possible, both positive and negative situations. This way they can test their competence in different areas. Failure in adolescence is good. Failure is where teenagers learn to be prepared or to make more of an effort.'

ANNIE ASHDOWN ON UNCOVERING NEGATIVE BELIEFS ABOUT CONFIDENCE

Confidence coach Annie Ashdown believes that confidence is for the most part learned by the majority of us. 'Biological predispositions, childhood experiences, our parents' perspectives and outlooks, the influence of culture and society, are all contributing factors. Often those who have been bullied as children, by classmates or family members, criticized by teachers, or continually undermined will lack confidence.'

You might feel that if only your background was different you would be more confident today; but as Ashdown points out, she went to a private school and used to suffer from low confidence, and her clients who are public-school educated are just as likely to have confidence issues as those state educated. 'School environments can easily undo confidence given by family,' she says. Gaining confidence is as much about unlearning what we've learnt about confidence. Remember lack of confidence often stems from practised learned behaviours. Don't make it about you being defected, that's far from the truth.

Ashdown says, 'From zero to aged 5 we are fed a lot of information without our knowledge. It's like having a tape recorder fitted into our inner circuit box we don't know about.' Uncovering and reframing these 'tapes' rather than being angry is the key to releasing negative beliefs dumped in your brain. 'We must remember that parents and teachers teach what they know,' says Ashdown. 'We need to ask ourselves: who taught from love but didn't approve of themselves?' When your 'committee' tells you that you are not good enough, ask yourself 'whose voice is it?' Remember firstly, it's untrue, and secondly, it certainly doesn't stem from you!

'Identifying whether someone eroded our confidence out of ignorance, misplaced love or cruelty is a big step in moving forward.'

YOUR HORMONES AND CONFIDENCE

Women might feel frustrated because men appear to have the edge on confidence. Well in a way they do. The male hormone testosterone fuels confidence, though as you'll find out in Chapter 8 (What kind of confidence do you aspire to?) this might not necessarily be the kind of confidence you would like, or the type of confidence that is right for you. You may have ample testosterone as a man yet feel your confidence is more of a front.

One of the most underestimated factors affecting women's confidence is hormonal changes, including the menstrual cycle, and changes in oestrogen and progesterone levels. Such changes affect how women's bodies react to their environment and influence the way they function.

> **"There are weeks when we can feel out of control and our confidence level goes down and we feel we can't handle things."**
>
> Dr Nitasha Buldeo, research scientist

When we're talking *real* confidence, one gender is not necessarily more confident than the other. Isn't the point of physiology that everything including psychology is based on biology? Not exactly. As Buldeo explains, biology is affected by the environment too. What this means is that we all have an underlying neural network – our inherent biology. 'So if as a child you are told you're doing well, then you will shine, and the neural network will spark up,' says Buldeo. How could those super-confident yet terrible singers auditioning for a place on the *X-Factor* not know they can't sing? It's because their mums may have fired up their neural networks by praising them too much.

REAL PEOPLE

"I lost my confidence as a teenager" – *Chris*

Chris can pinpoint the exact time in his life when he lost confidence: as a teenager at school. His parents were keen to give both their sons the best education and were immensely proud that Chris made it into a prestigious public school. Ironically his older brother, who wasn't bright academically, went to the state local and was happy. Chris on the other hand felt he was picked on. He couldn't say he was actually bullied, as being tall and muscular meant he could assert himself and put on a confident front. He didn't let others see he was upset by their comments.

During university, Chris didn't feel any better. He suffered from low self-esteem, yet managed to come across as an entertainer. He felt let down in all his friendships and relationships and envied his brother who had trained to be a chef and had a steady girlfriend.

It wouldn't have occurred to anyone that Chris lacked confidence because of his height and his outgoing personality. He landed a job in finance, not because he particularly wanted a job in this field, but because he had the right personality to sail through the interview for a well-paid job. On the surface he was like any young man, going out, drinking too much, having a great time. It was his brother who pointed out that Chris either felt used by people or picked on.

The best thing that happened to Chris was a breakdown last year, aged 27, as he then confronted his lack of confidence. His therapist helped him realize that he was a confident, happy child, and he could be that person again as an adult. His favourite activity as a child was writing stories and getting his friends to act them out. He recently started a scriptwriting course and found a job in the council. Every day he feels a little better.

You may be wondering having read this chapter what your inherent confidence is. If a proportion of our personality is biological and genetic, if this is who we are, then how do we know whether to accept this or change it? When does our inherent 'it' become a problem? If you're reading this book, then you've identified the answer to these questions and taken a positive move: to change something about you that in some way is making you unhappy. This doesn't mean that you will reject who you are naturally, especially as you will also now have absorbed that regardless of what your genetic confidence profile is, it will have been influenced by everything around you. Your confidence profile will be a mix of your genetic and biological make-up combined with what you experienced growing up. Whether your early childhood experiences are positive or negative or a mix, what is significant is that this can be reversed later at any time, like right now.

ASK YOURSELF

Q Can you remember what you were like as a child?

Q Can you remember how you felt when you went to school? Did your teachers encourage you?

Q What were your teenage years like?

Q Did your confidence change from childhood to teenagehood?

Q Can you identify pivotal points in your life that affected your confidence?

WHAT KIND OF CONFIDENCE DO YOU HAVE?

In this test, you will discover what kind of confidence you generally exhibit and how that affects your life. Do you have an authentic style, are you bold? Are you ebullient or indecisive? And where did that confidence style stem from? Were you brought up in an encouraging, supportive household or were you left to your own devices? To evaluate what style of confidence you have, answer the questions below as honestly as you can.

Test by Catherine Maillard
Translated by Nora Mahony

QUESTION 1

What do you think of the saying, 'They didn't know it was impossible, so they did it'?

A. You'd respect anyone who followed it.
B. That's your motto.
C. 'Proverbs are hardly relevant these days, are they?'
D. 'That's a bit risky.'

QUESTION 2

When you have a difference of opinion with one of your colleagues, do you:

A. Negotiate.
B. Argue the point.
C. Catch them off-guard to rattle them.
D. Keep a low profile.

QUESTION 3

What do you have the most doubts about?

A. The world today.
B. Others.
C. Nothing.
D. Yourself.

QUESTION 4

What word do you most associate with money?

A. Security.
B. Possibility.
C. Power.
D. Greed.

QUESTION 5

How do your closest friends see you? As someone who is:

A. Thoughtful.
B. Creative.
C. A big mouth.
D. Fragile.

QUESTION 6

How do you get ahead in life?

A. By drawing on your experience.
B. By jumping right in.
C. With a lot of uncertainty.
D. By making yourself indispensable.

QUESTION 7

What helps to build your self-confidence?

A. The chance to show your true colours.
B. The opportunity to innovate.
C. The feeling of success.
D. Feeling valued.

QUESTION 8

Do you let yourself go where life takes you?

A. You have faith in the way life works.
B. You plan ahead, and are always ahead of the curve.
C. You consider life to be a battle to be won.
D. You often have the feeling of swimming against the current.

QUESTION 9

You've heard a rumour that could cast doubt on your plans for your career. How do you react?

A. You make new plans; you're not afraid of change.
B. You demand a meeting to see if the rumour is true.
C. You're furious; you're not about to sit back and take it.
D. You lose control, convinced that it will happen.

QUESTION 10

For you, speaking in public is:

A. Something that requires preparation.
B. Fun.
C. A chance to assert your authority.
D. Basically inconceivable.

QUESTION 11

At a conference on our changing society and climate, which topic would you want to debate?

A. Change yourself to change the world.
B. Imagining energy for the future.
C. Between economic performance and social cohesion: what place for man?
D. Simple, local, concrete: ideas to change everything.

QUESTION 12

For you, saying no is:

A. A way to respect yourself.
B. Second nature.
C. Hardly original.
D. Painful.

CONFIDENCE STYLE:

Mainly As:
Authentic

Dependable and true to yourself, you try to live up to your values. Well in touch with your needs, desires and fears, you show real confidence in yourself, and are very self-assured.

Your confidence in yourself is founded on a kind of inner security that you perhaps gained as a child alongside parents who loved and supported you. Your confidence could equally be the result of your work on yourself. Conscious of your worth and inner resources, you know how to draw on your experiences, both happy and sad.

Mainly Bs:
Bold

You forge ahead with natural enthusiasm. Your faith in life, coupled with a good dose of creativity and realism, gives you great freedom. You know how to win followers.

You are bold when it comes to standing up for what you believe. You were probably encouraged to excel as a child. You dare to act where others hesitate. However, you also need to consider your actions. Once in a while, take the time to ask yourself how to develop your expertise in areas where you are already talented. Doing so will make you more objective. True self-confidence also takes our limits into account.

Mainly Cs:
Brazen

You certainly display great confidence, to the point that it's hard not to notice you. As an adult, you seem very sure of yourself – perhaps too sure. Deep down, do you really trust in yourself, or do you need all eyes on you to make sure you exist? This might be the pendulum-swing of a child who didn't get enough attention. Otherwise, why would you try so hard in certain situations? Start to appreciate yourself for what you are, which is the key to true self-esteem. It's only a small step from recognising your value to valuing your real skills.

Mainly Ds:

Indecisive

You seem indecisive. You take the advice of others before making decisions. Speaking your mind is difficult. Negative remarks can be taken very much to heart. You swing between a fear of displeasing people and the fear of making the wrong choice. As a child you weren't allowed to think for yourself. You weren't listened to, nor did you get much support in terms of your needs, desires or feelings, so you got on with it as well as you could. As an adult, you lack the benchmarks to position yourself. Ultimately, you have more confidence in others than in yourself. It's never too late to feel supported and encouraged. However, a change of perspective begins within.

CHAPTER 5

WHAT CAN YOU DO WHEN YOUR LACK OF CONFIDENCE IS PARALYSING?

Hopefully, having read Part 1 of the book, completed the tests so far, answered the Ask Yourself questions, and reflected on where your lack of confidence comes from in Chapter 4, your view on confidence is beginning to change. Above all, we hope that your view of yourself is changing too.

It's possible that this change might be slower if lack of confidence is paralysing in some way. We know that gaining confidence in something new is going to be easier for you once you absorb the idea that developing new skills and trying step by step is the key. However, we also know that for some people, extra help is needed, which is why we've included this chapter. If you have a particular fear, like public speaking, which makes you go to pieces, we hope that this chapter will give you the tools to overcome this absence of confidence.

You may think that some personality types are more prone to a debilitating lack of confidence. Before buying this book you may have even concluded that your personality is prone to lack of confidence, and that it's your personality that's at fault. Perhaps you're convinced that being shy is the reason you can't make business presentations. Maybe you believe that having a big mouth gets you into trouble and ruins your relationships.

In fact there isn't such a thing as a personality type that's more or less likely to be confident. If you find social situations like parties an absolute ordeal, you might believe that outgoing personalities never lack confidence in groups of people. Well, yes, some outgoing people are confident, but some aren't. However, the outgoing person who isn't confident in a particular social situation might be better at covering this up. Have you considered why some of these outgoing people you admire drink a little too much alcohol at parties? Yes, they too might be feeling insecure. And your hilarious colleague who seems to wing every presentation by telling jokes? Does that colleague come across as calm and relaxed – or manic?

The point we really want to get across is that no personality is 'bad' when it comes to confidence. All of our experts agree on this, and there is ample research to support this too. In fact, no personality type in particular has a problem with acquiring confidence. None of the experts interviewed equate being an extrovert versus introvert, or outgoing versus shy, with true confidence and we'll be exploring this in more detail.

BREAKING THE MYTH ABOUT SHYNESS

Let's start with shyness. Being shy is about being preoccupied with the self and feeling self-conscious. You may be thinking that if you have been shy since childhood that's a bad thing, that shyness can't be good, and that surely shyness *is* a lack of confidence. We know from psychology that shyness begins around 18 months old when babies start to develop a sense of self. However, groundbreaking research in the mid-90s from leading child psychologist Dr Jerome Kagan at Harvard University found that 15–20 per cent of infants are born with what he called 'inhibited temperament'. They're the ones kicking their legs as babies when someone they don't know appears, or they hide away when they're toddlers. This gets labelled as shyness. They may or may not grow up shy, but even if they do, it's not about a lack of confidence. Let's say they (and this could be you) are not keen on strangers. Maybe they don't get a buzz from big groups of people and instead simply feel more comfortable with one or two people. Well, the other point about Kagan's research is that shyness isn't fixed. If you are in your 20s reading this, fretting because you're in your first job and you feel awkward, trust us. In a few years' time there's nothing to say you won't be in your element.

It's important to think about your circumstances and how these affect your behaviour. Kagan's further research and his book *The Three Cultures* (Cambridge University Press) looked at how biology, psychology and the humanities influence our understanding of human nature. In an interview with Amy Novotney for the *American Psychological Association*[1] in 2008, Kagan said neuroscience and psychological science aren't enough to explain and understand human behaviour. One has to know more about the history of the person and the situation they're in: 'A particular brain state can lead to different psychological states in different people acting in distinct situations.'

According to Kagan, we are all affected by history and culture. If you were born in a war zone then even if your genes are confident, being bombed every day will affect you. If you've been looking for work during a period of recession and haven't succeeded, your confidence levels will inevitably be affected. On the other hand, you may find, for example, that now we're emerging from the recession in the UK you still can't feel positive.

PUT YOUR WEAKNESSES ASIDE

When you're not feeling positive about yourself, the risk is that you label situations that make you feel exposed, anxious or fearful, as weaknesses. Fear of job interviews, fear of making a presentation, fear of filling in a tax return, fear of going to a party and not knowing anyone can become more entrenched as the years go by. But instead of getting stuck on being hopeless and unable to deal with your weakness(es) and putting it under the umbrella of your lack of confidence, there is another way round this.

Start with taking a detached look at your so-called weakness. Why is it important? Is it important? Do you really need to convert this 'weakness' into what you might consider a strength? If it's something that you loathe doing and makes you feel miserable, consider the alternatives. If you are terrified of public speaking (which is one of the biggest, most common fears), do you need to make public presentations? If this is part of your work, or if you need to do so in order to get promoted or to raise money for a charity close to your heart, then yes, there are concrete reasons to develop the skills to do it.

Note that we're not labelling this as a weakness but as something you will learn to do, step by step, to make your life better. But let's say you are anxious about having to make a speech at your best friend's wedding. You are absolutely terrified of speaking in public. You don't even like big groups, but you feel you have to. Well, do you? Yes, it would be lovely to make a speech at your best friend's wedding, but is there something else you can do instead?

The key is to work out whether what you perceive as a weakness affects others and/or how it affects you. It's possible to reframe lack of confidence as something you need to learn *or* as something you don't need to learn and for the moment can put aside. This is not about shelving responsibilities but being kind to yourself and not putting yourself under undue pressure. It's the difference between saying 'I'm useless at big parties' and 'I don't like big parties', 'I couldn't face going to the gym' and 'I don't like gyms'. And then adding 'I prefer ...': 'I prefer being with one or two people', 'I prefer going for a long walk.'

FIND WAYS TO RESPECT OTHERS SO THAT YOU LEARN TO RESPECT YOURSELF

By showing respect to others you cultivate the ability to show respect to yourself. By acknowledging others you will find that you begin to be more forgiving of yourself. Practising respect for others helps us develop humility – which all the experts interviewed for this book agree is a sign of real confidence.

Who in your life deserves respect? How can you demonstrate respect? Can you listen more intently? Can you ask questions? Can you learn from observing how this person behaves and lives?

PREPARATION CANCELS OUT LOW CONFIDENCE

The performers we admire for having the guts to get up there prepare rigorously. We know that Madonna is one of the most confident women on the planet – and we know that she's also hard-working and rehearses relentlessly. All performers, whether they are dancers, opera singers, pop stars or actors, prepare. As Patsy Rodenburg points out, no actor would go on stage without rigorous rehearsals for several weeks, and without warming up their voice and their body before each performance. This is part of how they learn to control fear and stress. Rodenburg recalls how her great mentor, Mary Soames, once described how her father, one of Britain's greatest prime ministers, Winston Churchill, used to walk up and down in his bedroom practising out loud those great speeches before he delivered them. All too often we get stuck in our fears and forget the obvious: is it total lack of confidence? Or is it lack of preparation?

66 Control comes with being prepared. 99

Patsy Rodenburg, OBE, voice and leadership coach

FROM PUBLIC SPEAKING TO FEAR OF DRIVING

With some activities, confidence is straightforward. Think about things that you do easily. You might be great at DIY, or maybe you can throw a meal together without looking at recipes. You're confident in these activities because you've done them a lot, so much so that you don't have to think. The fact that you can't do something new (which may also be demanding and complex) confidently is to be expected: it's new, demanding and complex. Add to this scenario the fact that a new job may depend on this, for example, or other people can witness how you get on, and there's even more stress.

66 In more demanding situations things are complex. In anything demanding we have a certain amount of fear and doubt that we bring to it. This is natural. 99

Niki Flacks, acting coach, psychologist, therapist

Flacks teaches actors physical body cues (based on neuroscience) to help them override nerves and fears. She explains that these cues apply to all of us. These aren't body language movements to mimic confidence, but ways to get your body to send messages to the brain.

Opening up your chest and arms as if you're about to reach out to give someone a hug sends a signal to the brain that you're not under attack. This is something you can do on your own, along with some breathing just before you go into a stressful situation to help you calm down. Remember, confidence means being calm. (See the following boxout from Niki Flacks, plus Chapter 10, for more on this.)

Anything you can do to help your mind and body relax will help you overcome the big fears. If you're going to yoga or Tai Chi classes or doing any body work, remember to take those benefits into the rest of your life. This can be easier said than done. You may find you fall asleep in the ten minutes' relaxation at the end of your yoga class but the next day you have a panic attack. It's because the next day you forgot to breathe. 'When we're fearful we tighten our bodies,' says Flacks.

In some cases fear is not only natural, it's justified. Being fearful can even be a great thing (yes really, keep reading). When Flacks trains corporate staff in how to overcome their fear of public speaking, the first thing she does is assure them they are normal and that in fact they'd be crazy not to be afraid. If you are terrified of public speaking you might have internalized this as you being bad at this skill. Yet there is absolutely no need to feel guilty. Your feelings are normal: 'You are afraid because you know that at that moment when you're making a presentation people are judging you and they are questioning whether you are worthy of their attention. In a situation of being judged we are terrified.' You'd be crazy not to be scared. This has nothing to do with your ability to succeed with your presentation.

> **"You are scared *because* you are smart enough to perceive the dangers. Fear gives us adrenaline which is energy, and that energy is a gift."**
>
> Niki Flacks, acting coach, psychologist, therapist

NIKI FLACKS ON DEALING WITH FEAR

'Set the stage for how important your fear is:

- Ask yourself: Does my life depend on this? If it doesn't, this is not a life and death thing, your life will not end. That takes some pressure off.

Tackle the fear in small stages:

- Try a few minutes at a time; keep adding to that, check up to 45 minutes maximum.

Plan something fun:

- Plan something wonderful to do immediately after each session of tackling the specific fear.
- Choose something that makes you feel so good your brain pairs the experience you fear with an experience you love.
- Associating the fear with something you enjoy like a massage or chocolate cake de-intensifies the level of anxiety.

Choose the right person to help you:

- Don't choose someone critical.
- If the fear is something like driving, don't choose a parent or a partner: they love you so much that your driving becomes about life and death for them.
- Invest time in finding the right teacher, mentor, friend to help you.
- Find someone who gets excited about your breakthroughs.

Ask yourself: what's the worst thing that can happen?

- With a fear of cooking, what's the worst thing that can happen? You burn everything.
- Ask yourself what you can do when the worst thing happens. In the case of burning everything you've cooked, you call a restaurant to deliver your favourite food.

- *If the fear is about friends not being your friends anymore, consider firing them!*

Is it fear or social perfectionism?

- *Do you have unrealistic expectations? Do you have critical voices telling you that you can't do this?*
- *Approach your social perfectionism from a different angle.*
- *Fear of cooking? See what happens if you set the table beautifully and serve hot dogs and baked beans. People will adore it.*

Find a baby step to take:

- *If you're terrified of cooking, make a hard-boiled egg.*
- *Identify what you want to conquer and then identify the baby step.*
- *Stop obsessing with the 'can't' whatever. Take a small action.*

Tackle public speaking through your armpits:

- *We tend to control nervousness with physical tension, but tightening muscles signals to the brain that we're under attack.*
- *One of the quickest ways to overcome nerves is to let our arms out and let our armpits breathe.*

Discard don't and do rules:

- *Avoid advice based on don't say um, don't pause, don't be dry, don't be boring, tell a joke, do this, do that. This makes you more fearful. Your brain has to remember all the don'ts and dos.*

Instruct your body when you are in a state of fear:

- *Say out loud that you are scared whilst opening up your arms. Take deep breaths.*

- *SMILE. When you smile the muscles in the face can relax and this helps the fear in our brain subside.*

Assess how you feel after you've tried something:
- *Did it feel good, or easy, or not so bad?*
- *Did you feel 'wow I did it', 'wow, I didn't die'?*
- *Did you realize a light didn't go on over your head when you forgot something – and no one noticed?*
- *Remember, we learn by doing.'*

WHY PROFESSIONAL HELP HELPS

Just as you need a plumber to fix your broken boiler, or you look at a specialist website or a solicitor for legal advice, you may need a professional who has the qualifications and skills to guide you to overcome your fears. Not seeking specialist help makes life much harder for you. You could probably Google 'how to fix my boiler' and find instructions, but you don't because you instinctively know a plumber is needed. What you also need to learn to identify is when you can benefit from expert help.

Many people you admire for their fearlessness have taken risks and made dramatic life changes through professional help.

There are several reasons for seeking professional help when it comes to finding the confidence to tackle fears. Specialists from driving instructors to public speaking coaches have the expertise that family and friends are unlikely to have. At one extreme, friends and family might be used to the fearful you, and at the other extreme they might be too nervous to upset you by being honest. Another reason is that someone qualified can help in a constructive way. Many counsellors, therapists and coaches have themselves overcome fear so they are likely to be empathetic. Annie Ashdown became a coach having hired one during a period of meltdown when she felt she was falling apart and also knew she wanted to make a career change that would involve helping people. The fact that she empathizes with lack of confidence is what makes clients overcome any resistance. They realize she's 'been there', she knows what they are going through.

There are different types of professional help available, so take some time to work out what you need. If there is a particular skill you need, find the right person. If you need somebody to inject you with willpower and steer you to making changes, some life coaching may be work for you. If it's negative thought patterns that are paralysing you, then a good therapist will help you break those destructive patterns. A skilled, specialist therapist will help you get back to believing that you can master a given situation, because this is our innate human nature ever since we manage to walk as toddlers.

If you have chronic low self-image and low confidence, tackling this on your own is immensely difficult. As Flacks explains, it's unlikely that the world around you is helping you. 'If you don't smile, people don't smile at you. If you're not doing well then school, college, or your employer will reinforce your image as a loser. Good therapy should unhinge all the negative thought patterns so that you can create new behaviours that will gain more positive feedback.'

DR NITASHA BULDEO ON UNDERSTANDING WHAT YOUR BODY TELLS YOU

'Some people insist they are not confident despite having the knowledge to deal with a certain situation, but once they're in that situation, they're fine. Research scientist Dr Nitasha Buldeo explains that what's happening here is that their physiology perceives threats that don't exist. This is where some simple body awareness and calming breathing techniques help.

Listen to your body, become aware of what's going on inside. What's the sensation in your gut? Do you have sudden bowel urges? Are you breaking out into a sweat? By paying attention you know if it's something you can handle. By breathing correctly you can bring your heart rate down in a couple of minutes.

Figure out whether anxiety is lack of confidence or something else. *If your body and mind don't respond to taking in more oxygen this can indicate that there's a deeper problem that requires help and medication. Be sure to seek medical advice. The talking therapies work for something that is cognitive. If you get yourself into a state thinking about a fear, then cognitive therapy will work. But if the problem is physiological, talking alone won't work. We're now looking at how we can teach people to pay attention to the body so they can recognize the signs and avoid getting stuck in a place where drugs are needed.'*

KEEP GOING

Instead of making assumptions that other people don't have your problem because their personalities are different to yours, focus on your own journey. If you're driving you don't look at how everybody else is driving, otherwise you'll crash.

If you're able to progress step by step, you'll be able to let go of doing something perfectly without it going wrong, so the fear won't be paralysing. You'll be able to put aside the 'what-ifs' which Ashdown reminds us are down to years of negative conditioning that become rooted in our adult minds. Yes, it does get harder as we get older, and yes, year on year the internal mumbo-jumbo gets worse. The likelihood is you weren't born with these paralysing fears, but they developed. 'We start out fearless when we're young because we're naïve,' says Ashdown. 'And then we start to become crushed with other people's opinions and rejection. Accepting opinions is what crushes confidence. It's about learning to be who you are and to keep going. I now refuse to buy into others' negative beliefs and say "thanks for sharing your opinion, however, it's just that – an opinion and not a fact".'

We hope this chapter has given you ways to reframe extreme lack of confidence so that you view this in a different way. Accept your personality now that you know confidence is not related to any type of personality. Don't forget to relate how you feel to your circumstances. This isn't making excuses for yourself, this is being compassionate. If it's fear of losing your job, or actually losing your job, or a difficult boss that has eroded your confidence, this is not your fault. You haven't paralysed yourself, something external has injured you. If you have a deep-rooted problem, treat this as you would a physical or practical problem, and seek expert advice. The key is to keep going, keep trying, rather than giving up and avoiding.

ASK YOURSELF

Q Is there anything you are terrified of doing?

Q Which fears do you absolutely need to overcome? Which ones can you totally avoid anyway?

Q Are there situations in life you always avoid? What reason do you give, and what is the real reason?

Q Think of a specific activity you believe is beyond your abilities. Are you afraid, unprepared or lacking in the knowledge/skills needed for this activity?

Q Is there just one practical thing you can do to remove an obstacle so that you are free to work on overcoming fear? (E.g. paying a cleaner to deal with overwhelming mess in your home, finding a babysitter so that you have a free evening to take a course, exchanging skills with somebody so that you can both save money.)

DO YOU HAVE FAITH IN YOUR ABILITIES?

It's surprising, but self-confidence has nothing to do with success. On either end of the professional ladder, there are people who are sure of themselves, and those who aren't – and some of the most successful people can be the least confident and the least competent of people can seem the most confident. But as we're learning, if you focus on building your skills and working on your strengths you will naturally become more confident. In this test, let's look at how confident you are at work. Do you have faith in your abilities? Let's find out.

By Dominique François and Dominique Mazin, psychologist
Translated by Nora Mahony

QUESTION 1

Your company is celebrating an anniversary, and you've been asked to make a short speech.

D. Casting fail! They'll have to find someone else…

B. It's nice to have been asked. You're touched.

A. Not surprising. You love this sort of thing, and they know it.

C. Work, work and more work! They really have no idea…

QUESTION 2

Since the minute you took the floor at a meeting, one of your colleagues hasn't stopped smiling.

A. You ask him what has put him in such a good mood.

D. It throws you. He must think you're ridiculous.

B. You respond with a smile.

C. You look elsewhere, pretending to ignore him.

QUESTION 3

As you leave the office, a local radio journalist stops you to ask a few questions about stress at work.

B. You respond honestly.

C. Not a hope of debating this problem so close to your office.

D. You don't like answering journalists' questions.

A. If the journalist is nice, and the questions interesting, you'd accept doing the little interview.

QUESTION 4

Your interview just ended. As you leave, you're most likely to be thinking:

D. 'I should have said X and not Y!' You replay the entire interview in your head.

B. Fingers crossed! There's nothing to do now but wait for the verdict.

A. Yet again, I worked myself up for nothing. It wasn't that tough.

C. You go through the pros and cons on both sides: was the interview well run? Did I respond clearly?

QUESTION 5

You've been in the same office for five years and your boss still gets your name wrong.

A. You can't put up with that! You correct him every time.

D. Doesn't matter at all. You don't even notice anymore.

B. You give him a dose of his own medicine, and bungle his name right back.

C. You look down your nose at him. As far as you're concerned, he's a few sandwiches short of a picnic.

QUESTION 6

When you have an important professional phone call to make:

B. You take notes to stay clear-headed and not forget anything.

C. You concentrate for a few minutes before dialling the number.

D. Sometimes you will dial and then hang up.

A. You set a specific time for the call, and phone without hesitation.

QUESTION 7

You pass your boss in the hallway. He asks you to step into his office for five minutes.

D. 'Why? What's going on?' You can smell danger on the horizon.

B. If it were important, he would have called ahead to ask you to his office. So you go in, fairly calmly.

C. Why five minutes? It's strange to give the duration of the meeting but not the reason for it. You mull it over.

A. You follow him in without a second thought.

QUESTION 8

Thanks to an indiscretion, you have learned that your boss is leaving. It'd be great if you got his job!

B. You try to manoeuvre cleverly to achieve the desired result.

C. You ask the person concerned to confirm your boss' imminent departure.

A. You inform your boss (or the HR team) that you are applying for the job.

D. You wait. There's no sense in using information that isn't official.

QUESTION 9

In all honesty, the most important thing in choosing a job is:

B. Salary.

D. Working environment.

C. The focus of the work.

A. The possibilities of advancement.

QUESTION 10

You are one of two candidates for a sought-after position. The manager asks you in front of the competition, 'Why you rather than him/her?'

C. It's not your job to rule out the other candidate. You refuse to badmouth them.

B. You try to respond, awkwardly, by highlighting your best qualities.

A. You play the game! You try to be persuasive.

D. You stammer out a few words. You're already out of the running, as far as you're concerned.

QUESTION 11

When you have to contribute at a meeting...

B. You always refer to your notes, or even read them.

A. You usually speak without looking at your papers.

D. You're always ill at ease, and it shows!

C. Your audience thinks you're relaxed – but you're not.

QUESTION 12

Your boss, who is ill, begs you to take an important meeting for him. He's handing over the reins, and the make-or-break deal is all yours.

D. No way! It's too risky. You try to convince him that this isn't a good solution.

B. He really thinks you're up to it? You want to hear him say it – and repeat it – before you'd accept.

A. Not a minute to waste. You prepare for the meeting and research everything. You *must* be up to the challenge.

C. Seeing as you have no choice, you'll do it and do it right. But the *stress…*

***

Mostly As

You feel mostly confident

Like everyone else, you've been known to lose your momentum and doubt your abilities at times, but it never lasts very long. Your pride ensures that you find the necessary resources to achieve your goals and show what you are capable of. In fact, you seem to need to make sure that in some areas, you are a little better than others. Perhaps you felt that you weren't sufficiently recognised or valued during a certain time in your life, and now you're trying to prove them wrong. Others can be inspired by your success provided that you recognise their qualities – and occasionally your own weaknesses too…

Mostly Bs

You have to believe in yourself

If you want to make your way in the world, you have no choice but to believe in yourself, that's how you see it. Other people aren't going to fight your battles for you, or sing your praises. So it's up to you to give yourself the right opportunities to show that you're up to the challenges that work throws at you.

So you strive to behave responsibly by ensuring that your role is not open to question. When times get tough, you need to convince yourself, repeating that you have all the skills required to for the job, even if you sometimes doubt it.

Mostly Cs

You look good but feel like a fake

You know how to hide your doubts and weaknesses and appear to have confidence in yourself. In reality, this is just a façade behind which lurk some insecurities. You may have to work to convince yourself that you will stay the course, and you have moments of genuine concern. When you're afraid of not being up to it, you do everything in your power to prevent it from showing. Why? Perhaps is it a matter of pride or a certain mistrust of others, as if you fear that your weaknesses will be used against you. Try not to doubt yourself and others so much.

Mostly Ds

You doubt yourself constantly

You go to great lengths to overcome your lack of self-confidence but you doubt yourself constantly. This tendency to question yourself is painful to live with because you feel constantly judged. What are you afraid of? Not being appreciated or loved? Don't give up, and work to transform this weakness into a strength. Not feeling superior to others allows you to develop qualities of tolerance, empathy and good listening skills, which can be extremely useful in the working world. Think of how you can best use these resources.

CHAPTER 6

CONFIDENCE ROBBERS

O ne of our goals with this book is to help you understand that gaining confidence doesn't have to be complicated. It's possible to increase your confidence without making any radical changes to your behaviour just by being aware of the factors that affect your confidence in a negative way.

By being aware of what robs you of confidence, you can stay on track in developing skills that will help you gain confidence in a specific area. Just as children need to learn how to cross the road safely, we adults need guidance in how to make demanding journeys. Some of what we've identified for you may be obvious (for example negative people), but we want to explain exactly how confidence can be affected. Other factors we've pinpointed may surprise you.

Start with becoming aware of which of the following apply to you, and to what degree. The Ask Yourself questions at the end will then help you analyse yourself more. With some of these confidence robbers, awareness alone will help you steer clear (for example from negative people) and in other cases that are connected to your lifestyle (like exhaustion), you will need to evaluate how to handle this.

1. CONFIDENCE AS A GOAL

> **❝ Instead of aiming to do something more confidently, focus on the action and commit to doing it more completely or differently. ❞**
>
> Niki Flacks, acting coach, psychologist, therapist

Now you might not expect this as a confidence robber from a book called *Real Confidence*. Yet, bearing in mind our focus is on the real you and encouraging you to focus on the process of step by step accomplishing something you want, your goal is that something, as opposed to confidence itself. That something might be finding a new relationship, finding a new job, finding new friends. If you stay in the mindset of 'I'm just not confident enough to find a new partner/job/ friends' and hope to reverse that with 'I want to be confident enough to find a new partner/job/friends', all you are doing is reinforcing your belief that you lack confidence.

As a psychologist and therapist, Niki Flacks underlines that if confidence is the goal, embedded in this goal is a negative: that you are not confident. The key is to find actions. For a new relationship you might ask yourself whether it's best for you to try online dating, and take advice from friends who have navigated this successfully, or perhaps asking friends to introduce you someone they know might feel better for you. For a new job, you might set yourself a weekly target of job applications and/or learn new skills. For new friends, you might take evening courses in subjects you're interested in or join a networking group. Do things.

Banish confidence as a goal.

2. CONSTANT NEGATIVE THINKING

This is where you need to step back and listen to the yadda-yadda in your brain. If it's a constant stream of negativity, this is like a fence around your brain: you can't get to sorting out the overgrown weeds from the brambles until you break down the fence and get in there to do some gardening. Unfortunately our own beliefs and thought processes can be our biggest confidence robbers. It's like trying to cycle uphill with a bike that's got loose pedals. You never muster enough grip to get going and always have a sense of sliding back.

Face up to your pattern of negative thinking (so that awareness helps you to change it).

> **❝ *I am useless, I am nothing, I am hopeless* – this habitual negative thinking makes us feel worse. ❞**
>
> Dr Ilona Boniwell, positive psychologist

3. NEGATIVE PEOPLE

We all know someone who makes us feel drained or feel bad about ourselves – or both. Banish the guilt about avoiding such persons because there is ample good and scientific reason to do so. Our brains contain what are known in neuroscience as mirror neurons. 'This is why we feel what other people are feeling,' explains research scientist Dr Nitasha Buldeo. 'If I feel sad those neurons will highlight areas in your brain. Buddhist meditation works by turning this into something positive: everyone reflects the same thing to create peace. The Buddhists know that if one person in a group is experiencing another emotion it will affect the entire group.'

What we need to be aware of is how these mirror neurons affect us on a daily basis. Essentially spending time with negative people will make you negative. Identifying how being with a particular person (or group of people) affects you physiologically is the key to identifying who may not be good for you. Watch out for sensing your heart rate increase, getting headaches, feeling jittery and uncomfortable.

If you are that sad or broken person and you know deep down you're the negative one, find people who are working on themselves to be with in order to break through this. Perhaps they are going to therapy or reading books like this or making changes in their lives. Being with people like this will help you overcome your negativity.

Aim to hang out with content, relaxed people rather than anyone who moans.

4. PEOPLE WHO INSTRUCT YOU TO BE CONFIDENT

You are entirely justified in feeling terrible when anyone tells you to 'just' be confident, or worse still thinks that instructing you to be confident is in any way helpful or encouraging. It's not. Unfortunately it's often people close to us who say these things. If that's the case, you may need to reassess how helpful it is to see that particular friend who tells you how to be.

❝ It's one of the silliest things you can say to someone: be confident, think confident. Being told this isn't helpful. All it can do is make you feel bad, because you can't will yourself to be more confident. And then you feel there's something wrong with you. We don't learn anything from someone telling us how to feel. ❞

Niki Flacks, acting coach, psychologist, therapist

For long-term unemployed people, mums wanting to return to work but feeling their skills are out of date, and anyone dealing with the blow of redundancy, some training schemes can ironically have a similar effect by telling candidates to be confident at interviews. That's because they're not working from within. Confidence coach Annie Ashdown says that superficial confidence techniques don't help people who are unemployed or have been made redundant. 'It's absolutely pointless telling someone to behave confidently in job interviews if inside they feel bad about themselves. Change has to come from the inside.'

Seek out support from people who are able to listen.

5. POSITIVE AFFIRMATIONS

You might be stunned to read that positive affirmations can rob you of confidence. This may even sound like a contradiction when we've told you in previous chapters to ditch negative thinking and negative people. We think positive affirmations can be great. But not right now for developing your confidence. We suspect you may have already tried this and may have tortured yourself over why telling yourself you are confident doesn't work. Well, no amount of visualization, no compiling dream lists, no pretending to be your ideal self will fix your confidence.

Psychologists are damning about these methods and with good reason. There is no scientific evidence for them. The biggest study led by one of the most respected psychologists, Dr Roy Baumeister,[1] showed that when you try to build up self-esteem, the result can be artificial without producing better results or higher performance. It's not real. Repeating 'I am confident' doesn't make the slightest bit of difference. There may be a place for all these methods but *not* for tackling confidence.

Accept yourself just as you are – that's the most positive way to affirm your real self.

> **❝All the research shows that people with high self-esteem who use positive affirmations develop *higher* self-esteem. But for people with *low* self-esteem positive affirmations have the opposite effect. Their self-esteem is reduced even more.❞**
>
> Dr Ilona Boniwell, positive psychologist

6. THE GLAZED FAKE SMILE

You may have developed a fixed smile as a coping strategy for dealing with difficult people, especially at work. The problem is that a glazed fake smile then becomes a default setting. In any situation where you feel uncomfortable, whether it's complaining about service in a store or going on a job interview, you'll be so used to that glazed smile that you won't even realize it's not real. But by real (confidence), we really do mean real. When the difficult people you're dealing with are more than difficult and are perhaps bullies, this has a particularly detrimental effect. 'If we smile at bullies and are nice to them we are rewarding them,' says Annie Ashdown. 'It erodes self-confidence.'

7. ACTING CONFIDENT

You may have been told endlessly to 'fake it until you make it'. For some people this is easy and even preferable to developing real skills. Ironically, over-confident people can fake confidence because, not being concerned with competence and perhaps being on the narcissistic side, they don't care. But trying to fake confidence when you suffer from chronic lack of confidence can be absolutely terrifying. (More on over-confidence in Chapter 8.)

Faking confidence is immensely stressful on the body, so you wouldn't want to put yourself through this anyway. What we know from medical science is that the heart rate goes up, there is increased acid in the body and a host of stomach and bowel conditions can develop as a result.

Keep trying until you make it.

> **The stress of trying to do more than you honestly know you are capable of doing is not good for your health. And it's not real confidence.**
>
> Dr Nitasha Buldeo, research scientist

8. OVER-ANALYSING THE PAST

While therapy has its place, over-analysing the past can stop you transforming the present. Confidence issues are difficult to break through, so on the one hand you are tempted to figure out why you lack confidence, but on the other hand you don't want to dwell on the past.

Let's say you've always known that a critical mother has been at the root of your lack of confidence. Well, you know this. We hope that through Chapter 4 you may have evaluated other reasons too for how you are. But if you restrict yourself to the past and revisit this every day, it's as if you reinforce in your mind that you're doomed. 'That's a life sentence,' says Niki Flacks.

There are different types of therapy, and if you feel drawn to therapy it's a good idea to consider which type and which therapist can help you best. Developing confidence involves actively working on your mind right now, so it's worth considering whether right now is the right time to revisit the past. If you need confidence to overcome losing your job so that you can find another job, now might not be the right time to be talking about how you feel you've been rejected since you were a child. You can always come back to healing wounds, from a stronger vantage point.

The likelihood is that you have lots of messages in your head that you've absorbed from the past, and you need to shut these down in order to gain confidence. To shut down these tapes Flacks recommends staying rooted in the present – reminding yourself no one is criticizing you this minute: 'Then take action. DO something physical. Obviously a yoga class, running, dancing, any pleasurable physical activity would be best. However, just going for a ten minute walk will get you "out of your head" and into your body. After this you will feel better and think more clearly. The negative messages won't have as strong a hold on you.'

So put on some music and do something that gives you pleasure, giving yourself a challenge that makes this activity harder. It could be anything from DIY to baking, sewing to gardening. Lose yourself in the moment and the negativity will be lost too.

9. COMPARING AND DESPAIRING

OK, you know this one makes you feel bad, but we have to remind you. With social media playing such a huge part in our lives there's even more temptation to go through peoples' timelines and photos, comparing them with your own life and despairing. This is dangerous as it feeds the negative thinking in your head (why don't I have a better job, why am I single, why can't I get my life together?). If you're feeling inadequate and insecure, comparing yourself with others can make you feel worse. Your negative thinking then starts forming into beliefs that other people are better than you in some way. As Ashdown explains, this is dangerous: 'We don't feeling worthy of success or happiness.'

Restrict your time on social media.

10. AN EASY LIFE

If you feel that a hard life has robbed you of confidence, this may make you feel better. A fantastic childhood and education, and not having any real challenges, can actually have the reverse effect on confidence. 'Look at teenagers now coming out of their parental home feeling lost,' says Boniwell. 'The more spoilt they are with easy access to branded clothes and luxury holidays, the less confident they are dealing real life problems. This is why more and more children are staying at home well into their 20s. They expect too much without having gained enough competence to go out and maintain the standard for themselves. So they sit at home and do nothing.'

Acknowledge that your past has made you strong.

11. EXHAUSTION

Avoid at all costs reaching a point of being so tired you cannot function. Buldeo warns that when the body gets exhausted, the resources in the mind also become depleted. When the brain is exhausted its circuitry gets cranky. That means your mind won't be up to learning new skills so that you can master new situations and become confident. If you're a bit of a workaholic and can't tell when you're exhausted, watch out for cravings as that's the brain screaming out for glucose/energy so it can operate directions for all the body's functions.

Sleep, rest and play.

12. DRINKING ALCOHOL TO DE-STRESS

No one is going to deny that the odd drink is relaxing. But if you find that you need to drink in order to de-stress at the end of a demanding day, there are some side-effects to bear in mind. The autonomic system in our brain (which looks after functions in our body including the heart) goes into overdrive when we're over-tired. 'When the autonomic system is in overdrive the body becomes acidic. The nerves are firing, the heart rate goes up, and there's hyper tension,' explains Buldeo. None of this is good for the body, and needless to say alcohol doesn't help. The addition of alcohol also affects the brain. 'Alcohol numbs and shuts down the frontal lobe of the brain which is the part thinking about stress and how bad we feel about ourselves, so we're numbing our self-awareness.' This means that if you drink because you're exhausted from work but want to find the confidence to change careers, by numbing the stress you're also numbing what will help you make the change.

'For those people who feel they need alcohol to de-stress, one of the most important things they can do to help themselves is to start having a diet that's very high in green vegetables, as the alkalizing effect will help them limit alcohol,' says Buldeo. 'Avoiding acidic foods and eating alkaline and alkalizing foods will help.'

Find a relaxation technique or class like yoga to help you relax.

13. MODERN CITY LIFE

Modern city life might seem exciting in many ways, but it has a surprising effect on inner reserves of confidence. When day after day you are on the treadmill of commuting, working long hours, hunched up over computer screens, not to mention being inside a lot with our long, wet and cold winters, your body and mind get used to an impersonal environment. If you are new to a city and still finding your way, most of your social contact might be online. Or you may be working long hours and not have time to see your friends. Add to this the fact that at weekends you might feel wiped out and meeting up with people you know across the other side of town might be impractical. What tends to happen is that we get used to this way of living, and may not even be aware of the how it affects us, particularly if we're pleased we have the job and we're enjoying other benefits to being in a city – like educational or cultural opportunities. It is important, however, to be aware of how city life can affect us.

> ❝ We get deadened in cities. We look at pavements and floors. We're not fully alert and present. We close ourselves and go into our bubble. ❞

Patsy Rodenburg, OBE, voice and leadership coach

Going into a bubble might be OK for a while, but you can't sustain it. If you're always staring at your phone and unaware of who and what is around you, not only are you losing the ability to connect with what's around you, you're also losing the ability to connect with yourself. It's a terrible cycle because firstly community is about forging connections. Lack of community in cities is basically lack of people making connections. As Rodenburg explains, this lack of community robs us of confidence on a deeper level: we don't feel protected, safe and secure. 'If we're all present with each other we're also safer. It's hard to commit a crime against someone you know.'

To develop real confidence you need to know the real you, so you need to be connecting with the real you. And the real you is not in the pavement or inside your phone.

Stop using your smartphone when you walk on the street and be fully aware of walking in the city.

14. DIFFICULT PEOPLE

66 Build up the confidence to stand up, show up and speak up. 99

Annie Ashdown, confidence coach

One of the biggest knocks to your confidence is difficult people, and unfortunately they are everywhere: at work, in your social network or your family. What tends to happen is that lack of confidence prevents you from setting firm boundaries with others about what is and isn't acceptable behaviour. This lack of boundaries signals to difficult and dominant people that they are free to undermine you. Ashdown reminds us of the Buddhist principle to be like a willow tree: solid, rooted, with flowing flexible leaves. How to put that into practice? Difficult people are predictable so you can at least plan to deal with them.

One way to set boundaries is what Ashdown calls 'fogging': agree and deflect. Let's say you're trying to find the confidence to follow your dream of setting up a new business. Then a parent tells you they heard on the radio that most people who leave their secure job to set up a business end up regretting this. Instead of getting angry or defensive or upset take a deep breath (if necessary count to 10) and say: 'Thanks for your input. Where shall we have tea?' (This works particularly in family situations.) By being prepared you can also prevent difficult people from undermining you or getting to you.

Write down some punchy short phrases aimed at difficult people in your life and practise saying them out loud.

15. STAYING STUCK

Holding back in life and staying stuck in the safety of what's familiar in terms of relationships, homes, jobs and friends, keeps us stuck in our minds too. Think of how bored you become with the routine of commuting to work and how excited you are the day you head to the airport for a holiday. Change from our routine helps us remember who we are and what we want in life. Think of being relaxed on holiday and how you find yourself having conversations about making changes in your life, whether it's small ones like eating more healthily or big ones like moving.

The problem with being stuck, however, is that it's like being in a long, dark tunnel. You can't see a way out. The first thing is to acknowledge that you are stuck, without blaming anyone or any situation. It's hard enough feeling like this, without adding to it with more negativity. Don't expect to make major changes immediately. Be gentle with yourself.

It's small changes like choosing something different for lunch or going home a different way that can slowly get you into the mood for change. You'll find that small new choices will gradually lead to small changes.

> 66 **If something doesn't work, try something else, and then move on again. Be more flexible, embrace impermanence.** 99
>
> Dawn Breslin, confidence coach

Every day this month, change just one detail in your daily routine.

DAWN BRESLIN ON THE IMPORTANCE OF BALANCE

'In our society we've developed a masculine energy mindset – we tell ourselves we can do anything we want so long as we take action. Our formula for success is to drive-drive-drive, push-push-push. This way of living is burning people out. I believe in our human evolution it is time to find our way back to balance.

When you've been through something like business failure or redundancy, pushing to find another business opportunity or job can be fatal. After the burn out of our energy, this period is certainly not the time to be doing one thing a day to get a job, or one thing a day to learn a new skill. If you push too hard you're likely to become ill. When you're depleted, it's probably ineffective to take on something new and start pushing.

In these situations we need to give ourselves permission to stop and be still. In ancient traditions, we learn about balance: yin and yang, and the 50–50 principle. In our society we are giving out 100 per cent and not resting, being, or reaching out for support when we need it.

When a child is exhausted we put that child to bed, we tend that child until the child's energy starts to return, and we let that child start to play a little, and then more, until the child feels ready. We are human just like children – our needs are the same.

This process of recovering from burnout is a bit like composting. From the dirty, stinking compost of our painful endings, new beginnings will emerge. Just like the seasons, our lives move in cycles, and over a period of time little seedlings make their way from the darkness of the undergrowth towards the light as they begin to grow. We cannot force new beginnings; they take place naturally and organically. It's seen as weak to take time out and to be gentle with ourselves, but it's essential to rebalance exhaustion in order to regain our confidence.

If we step back we can find ways to slow our lives down. Evaluate your circumstances and find a way to minimize outgoings. That could mean cutting down on spending or downsizing. Find a way to cover what you need while you recover and repair. I gave myself two years to recover from burnout. I simplified my life and had just enough financially to get by.

To reactivate your confidence post-job loss, forget work for a while and focus on how you want to feel every day. Think of five feelings you would love to feel and ask yourself how you could weave these five words into different aspects of your life. If you would like to feel wonder, then go meander somewhere beautiful. Curiosity? Go explore somewhere new.'

REAL PEOPLE
"I feel better today" – Marina

Two decades after leaving university, Marina was living in a damp, horrid bedsit with mice, in an inner city area with aggressive gangs of bored youths, and with no friends. Divorce, wrong financial decisions (spending her modest divorce settlement on travelling and then setting up a business that failed in India) and the recession all contributed to her demise. She settled for a low-paid catering job and despite getting ill didn't dare take time off because she couldn't afford to. By the time she lost this job too, all that swirled in her head was a litany of 'I am useless, I have made a mess of my life, no one understands me, what's the point of living.' She believed she was incapable of doing anything.

A chance invitation from an old friend who didn't give up on her proved to be the catalyst she needed. Could Marina go and house sit and look after the dog whilst her friend travelled? Marina decided to take a break from rock bottom.

The house was by the beach in a peaceful place in Cornwall. To begin with Marina took the dog for walks and cried on the windswept beach. Then the dog tempted her to go in different directions, the sun danced out, and she explored more. Now in her head she heard 'I feel better today, I feel better now'. She started to say hi to people. She started to explore the cafes. When her friend texted to ask if everything was OK, she went from replying about the dog to replying about herself. 'You're sounding so much better,' texted her friend. 'You don't have to go back to London. Just a thought.'

Fast forward: Marina found an admin job for a local charity and a house share in Cornwall. She started a photography blog and an Instagram account. And there's a lovely, loving man on the scene now too.

We hope this chapter has given you food for thought and that you may even smile just a little bit when you recognize any of our 15 confidence robbers as they appear in your life. We've aimed to explain how something erodes your confidence as well as how to avoid it. Obviously some of these will be easier than others. You can totally pass on acting confident and faking a smile, for example, and that will be a relief. You can probably avoid Moany-Mary at work, but tackling a negative relative will require more preparation.

You can make a point of pampering yourself at home so you don't get exhausted, but cutting out wine at the end of a stressful day may be a hard habit to break. There's no need to put yourself under any pressure. We're not asking you to compile lists and goals and give yourself time limits. This is about making the process of gaining confidence easier for you.

ASK YOURSELF

Q Do you lose confidence before or after being with certain people? Who are they?

Q Have you noticed that you start the day feeling reasonably OK but become less confident as the day goes on? What triggers your decreasing confidence?

Q What is it that people say that makes you aware that your confidence decreases? What phrases affect you?

Q Are you looking after yourself the best that you can? Are you resting and sleeping enough, eating well and actively thinking of your wellbeing?

Q Are there people around you who are moaning or negative? What is the balance of negative versus positive people in your daily life?

3 HOW CAN YOU LEARN TO BE CONFIDENT?

CHAPTER 7

IS CONFIDENCE A SKILL YOU CAN LEARN?

Yes.

There, that's the simple answer.

Not only can we develop confidence, there is evidence that this can be done at any stage of our lives. It really is never too late. One study in 2014 from Concordia University's Centre for Research in Human Development[1] examined self-esteem changes and confidence in adults over 60 over a period of four years. The study, published in the journal *Psychoneuroendocrinology*, showed that senior citizens who continue developing confidence have health benefits and suffer less from stress. If you think about this, you'll realize that working on your confidence is a good thing in more than one way because the process provides health benefits too. If you're young, well, the message is that you have the ample time. If you fear that it's not being young that gets in the way of you developing confidence, you can be assured that this isn't the case.

But perhaps the real question is something else. Let's say you manage to develop your low confidence into confidence – will it last? The thing is, confidence isn't a final goal post that we get to and that's it, we transform the post into a flag. For a start life is unpredictable and anything could knock us back. But if it's also in our very nature to master our environment, then true confidence will inevitably involve mastering something new. As toddlers we manage to walk and then have to run and then ride a bike ... As adults, if we're *truly* living, we'll be striving for something new, whether it's running a marathon, doing a headstand in yoga, reading the complete works of Charles Dickens, making every single Nigella chocolate recipe or making a speech at our best friend's wedding.

LOW CONFIDENCE IS A GREAT STARTING POINT

"Society has a narrative that under-confident is wrong and

that over-confident is good, but that's not the case. "

Dr Tomas Chamorro-Premuzic, Psychologist and Professor of Business Psychology at UCL

What Chamorro-Premuzic is recommending in the quote above is a change in your view of confidence. If you think of it as your ability to detect a risk and work out how to deal with this, you instantly shift away from having a negative view of yourself. Shifting from here to being proactive isn't so hard.

Let's say you put off driving on a motorway. You've never done it before, you're terrified of getting on and off the motorway, fear driving at a high speed and would panic about heavy goods vehicles. That's you identifying a threatening risky situation.

Of course you can manage the situation by avoiding the motorway altogether. Or, you can follow Chamorro-Premuzic's advice to focus on developing competence. With this example it might mean taking some extra driving lessons to cover the motorway, even though you've passed your test. You might also talk to experienced drivers and perhaps travel with them as a passenger to gain their tips.

ASK FOR FEEDBACK AND ADVICE

Dr Tomas Chamorro-Premuzic stresses the importance of developing self-awareness and working with what you have, along with keeping focus on a strong work ethic. Of course, feedback is only a booster if you choose to use this as an opportunity to improve your skills. Chamorro-Premuzic warns that most people get upset about feedback even when there is a scientific personality assessment. They resist changing what they need to in themselves.

Another approach is to seek out an older mentor to guide you. This could be somebody in your family, someone nurturing at your workplace or perhaps you've been to a course and the course leader is somebody you are able to keep in touch with. 'All the great leaders I have ever met have had fantastic, generous mentors,' says Patsy Rodenburg. 'When someone passes on to you their legacy that gives you a tremendous confidence.'

DR ILONA BONIWELL ON GAINING CONFIDENCE

'I used to feel very confident about cooking until I came to France. I thought I was very good at it. But I realized in France I didn't know how to cook at all. So it took me a few years to gain the confidence. When you invite people for lunch in France – my husband is French and has the French habit of inviting people over for lunch – you have to show effort and skill in everything you make.

You prepare all weekend. My husband didn't know a woman might not know how to cook according to the French standards, so it took him a while to figure out and then I went into panic mode when I had people over. I gained the confidence by first refusing to have people over for a while, and I practised a lot on my husband. I cooked things I thought I was fantastic at in England (like soups and casseroles) but these were too low key for France. He would say, no, you can't serve that. In France you have to learn how to cook properly, what to do with different types of meat, how to make dishes like 7-hour lamb with different spices. It's unforgiveable for meat to be dry, or not cooked properly, or not delicious. My range of dishes is still limited and I can still only serve easy options like côte de boeuf *in the oven, but I can do these well and they are acceptable.*

By taking little steps I'm gaining confidence. That's how confidence can be learnt. It's about the totality of little steps rather than one big change. I don't believe in miracles. I don't believe in 30 days to this and that changes.'

If there's a case study that illustrates that we can learn to be confident it's Boniwell herself, not because of managing her international work schedule, and five children between herself and second husband, but because she admits she cried over learning to cook for French people. As we can see from her account, the way she dealt with this was to approach it like a project, slowly and methodically, dish by dish. As a psychologist, of course Boniwell knows performance accomplishment is the number one source of self-efficacy, accounting for a whacking 70 per cent. This is important for all of us to know. If we want to master something new (or for that matter something old that's been bugging us) it's the little successes that lead us there. If you want to go from couch potato to super-fit it's going to be about building your fitness level week by week. Rather than focusing on the abstract idea of confidence, identify and focus on the skill you need to develop and gain competence in.

CONFIDENCE CAN BE DEVELOPED IN A PRACTICAL WAY

> **"Confidence is there somewhere – you've just got to release it. "**
>
> Patsy Rodenburg, OBE, voice and leadership coach

Performers do not train in confidence. Any performance training (acting, dance, music) consists of learning a set of skills that mastered and combined provide a solid foundation for performers. This is what gives them confidence; and maintaining and developing these skills maintains their confidence. It's the practical skills that are important as a basis. Similarly, for non-performers in 'performing' situations (like business presentations, speeches or managing teams), developing confidence can be approached in a practical way. If you can identify something practical to learn for any situation where you lack confidence, you'll find learning this subsequently develops your confidence.

PATSY RODENBURG ON DEVELOPING CONFIDENCE

'There are people who have a lot of knowledge but are shy. You have to teach them that they can speak out because they do have the knowledge. On the simplest level the work is very pragmatic. Teaching comes down to simple things in the body, like showing the connection between breath and the voice. It's about the body being centred and connected; it's about the breath being low so we can power the voice and the human spirit. All of this can be taught. However, it's not enough to say to someone put your chest out and be confident, that's hollow. It takes practice. A lot of practice.'

When acting coach Niki Flacks shows actors how to deal with audition nerves, she demonstrates the difference between arriving at an audition *acting* confident and arriving as one's true self, and asks the actors on the workshop to analyse the difference.

In the first version her face and body are taut and her voice is 'on'. She could be anybody and comes across more like a sales person. In the second version what's striking is that it's as if she's opened a window of vulnerability crossed with humility that makes her hugely appealing and interesting. Her voice isn't high pitched and fast, and there's a softness in her body. What's fascinating is that this could apply to absolutely anybody in a wide range of situations where confidence is needed: a job interview, a meeting with management, making a speech at a wedding or a funeral, going on a date, going to a networking event.

What Flacks impresses on actors is that confidence must first come from the baseline of their skills. These skills must then be maintained when they are 'resting' and doing other work to pay the bills. For actors this means keeping up with vocal and body exercises and memorizing lines. In an audition they must show themselves, rather than a fake confident version of themselves.

So what can non-actors be developing at all times to avoid presenting fake versions of themselves? Since this book is about real confidence, it's important to remember to connect with yourself, to know yourself, to accept yourself, and to be developing anything that you need to. You can't wait until the night before having to make a speech for a miracle confidence pill. You can't hope to wake up one day and be confident about getting out of a dead-end job. Developing skills related to the areas where you lack confidence is the key to developing the skill of confidence itself.

MOTIVATION IS THE GLUE BETWEEN CONFIDENCE AND YOU

Inevitably, someone who lacks confidence is full of self-doubt, and that doubt translates into helplessness over developing confidence. But international speaker and coach Dawn Breslin points to a missing link: motivation. This, she says, is the glue: 'It's like politicians missing the point when they say education is important: you can't just make kids want to study. What's going to *connect* them to learning?'

The point here, then, is that we need to figure out first what excites us, so that there's an incentive to develop confidence. It's not enough to just want to be confident in a given area, you need to be clear about your motivation. If you feel you're utterly hopeless in group situations, where you just can't think of anything to say and worry that everybody else is super-witty, what is your motivation here? Is it to be accepted, or to be one of the gang, or to get attention, or approval, or for your boss to see you as interesting? Let's say your motivation is to feel relaxed – then your approach might change. Perhaps all you need to do is find the courage to ask questions so that you become the listener in the group, the one people want to really talk to.

At any given stage you need to remember what you've accomplished before. Even if you're painfully shy with dating, can you remember playing as a kid? If you could play and connect with other children, then you can 'remember' how to connect with adults and feel more comfortable. Just because a particular environment or situation doesn't suit you now, doesn't mean that's who you are.

> ## **"That confidence muscle just needs to go to the gym again. It's our perception or a bad experience that makes us feel it's gone."**
>
> Dawn Breslin, confidence coach

The biggest problem that confidence expert Annie Ashdown identifies in turning low confidence to confidence is the stigma attached to having low confidence. She highlights the fact that although people tend to hide a book with a confidence title, there are many celebrities out there who openly hire confidence coaches. The point to make here, Ashdown emphasizes, is that these celebrities are saying 'I want to be better', rather than 'I am defective'.

There are many people who are confident and successful in one area who want to develop confidence in another area and who see this as part of their ongoing personal development. If you can look at developing confidence as extending your confidence into other parts of your life, then you make the process much more manageable. Keep reminding yourself that confident people are always striving to achieve a little bit more. Confident people are always identifying something they can improve on, something they can change, something new they can learn.

ACTION CHANGES YOUR BRAIN CHEMISTRY

It's not thinking about confidence that makes you more confident, but taking small steps, achieving small accomplishments, and slowly mastering something, whether it's cooking or running or driving. You've probably read somewhere that the brain is plastic and this is proof that we can change, but we bet you're wondering what this really means and how on earth it can apply to confidence and you. Well it doesn't mean that you can 'think yourself confident'. It's about the way the brain responds to actions – those small little actions that you are going to take.

It all goes back to neuropsychologist Donald Hebb, who discovered how the brain learns 50 years ago. His theories were summed up by neurobiologist Carla Shatz, who coined the phrase 'neurons that fire together wire together' meaning broadly that every time we think/do something it becomes embedded in our brain. Neuroscientists have been refining our understanding of how this works.

DR NITASHA BULDEO ON BREAKING HABITS

'What brain plasticity suggests is that all behaviour can be changed or altered. Constant activation of a particular network by repeating a behaviour results in that network becoming the default network. The slightest stimuli will initiate an impulse along this network resulting in almost automatic behaviour. This is the neuropsychology of habit formation.

So breaking a habit involves forming new neural connections. This involves consciously thinking about the new behavioural outcome and almost schooling yourself to perform the given task. With repetition this new behavioural network forms and becomes the default so the new behaviour is performed almost automatically.

The key here is that it's the physical action that forms the neural pathway. Just thinking about something does not always activate the motor centres of the brain that are engaged in physical action. To change a habit one has to engage in the new desired behaviour. This is a possible reason that professional sports people practise in an almost ritualistic fashion.

Reinforcing a [new] habit is about consistency, frequency and repetition. Taking charge, by consciously changing your behaviour, gives you a sense of hope as well as enabling you to learn more productive skills.'

Let's take driving as an example. Your brain learns to automatically associate putting your car key into the ignition switch with a whole series of movements and thoughts that are automatic. When you buy a new car or rent a car abroad, driving is a disorienting experience until you get used to the new car. Now let's say you decide you *will* start going to the gym. However, every time you get home feeling knackered after a bad day at work, you feel you just don't have the confidence and open a bottle of wine in front of the TV instead. Your untouched pristine gym kit triggers a bad feeling and the bottle of wine and TV becomes a habit. Right, so how do we go about forming a new habit?

Translated into daily life, this means first telling yourself you'll go to the gym with a colleague or friend straight after work on a Monday and a Wednesday instead of heading to the pub. On a Sunday and Tuesday night you prepare your gym kit after the news, listening to music whilst running a bath. You and your friend walk to the gym and catch up on gossip and have a laugh. You get home and have a healthy dinner. Eventually this becomes a routine.

Now the harder the new habit, the harder it is to form. Factoring in the difficulty of the task is not so simple because there are more factors to take into account, namely desire and resistance, which can motivate us or become an obstacle. For example, adding berries to our morning porridge is in no way the same as finding the confidence to start online dating after the break-up of a long-term relationship. Getting into the habit of going for a walk in the park for fresh air at lunchtime is not the same as developing the confidence to deliver presentations whilst suffering from a stammer. If you love berries it can take just three days to get organized and add them to your porridge. If you're working in a deskaholic environment it might take 13 days to make the walk in the park a daily office habit. If your dream is writing the next bestselling thriller it might take you 30 days (the figure most often bandied around) to get into a daily writing habit on your commute. But can we put a time frame on becoming confident when confidence is so complex?

Once you get your head round the fact that our brains are plastic and that it's actions that help us form new habits, you will find your approach changes. If you're in a negative routine that reinforces your lack of confidence, the longer this routine lasts, the harder it becomes to rewire. This doesn't mean that you have to get anxious and hard on yourself – the tiniest change you are able to make to a negative routine will have a positive effect, and these tiny changes will accumulate. If you hide in the corner of every single group situation and sneak out at the earliest opportunity, always remaining invisible, just moving along one chair and leaving a little after you'd normally leave will make a difference. Taking action to break a pattern is a positive process.

We hope of course that you also decide on a positive course of action: something new and exciting to master. Knowing that change is possible scientifically will motivate you to take those small actions that will rewire your brain.

REAL PEOPLE

"It didn't matter that I wasn't confident" *– Louisa*

Department store fashion buyer, Louisa, was going through a confidence crisis about her job and her life coming up to 30. 'I was working for a designer and I just didn't feel I fitted in that fashion-y world. I've got a slight problem with my feet which means I walk a bit funny, so I wasn't this graceful, stick thin girl. I tried going to a salsa class because I had this fantasy of dancing. A bloke told me not to follow like a lump of lead and then he mimicked my walk. I was crushed.'

When a friend she hadn't seen for years invited Louisa to her 30th birthday, she almost didn't go because there was a Lindy Hop class as part of the party. 'The thing is I've always wanted to dance but didn't have the confidence, because of the way I walked. But since I worked in fashion and I generally only met other women or gay men, I had promised myself that I would say yes to absolutely any invitation to anything non-fashion. I don't know if it was the cocktails but basically I didn't care that night that I was rubbish.'

From this party Louisa went on to take classes in Lindy Hop several times a week. All her holidays were dance course holidays. 'It didn't matter that I wasn't confident because I so wanted to do it, I found really encouraging teachers, there were others like me and we helped each other and became very good friends. People comment now and say I'm really confident dancing, but they have no idea how much work I've put into my hobby. It was worth it because my life changed and I found the confidence to change jobs.'

Whichever perspective we look at there is ample evidence that confidence is a skill that can be developed – if we focus on the skills that need to be developed. We're not going to advocate a quick-fix promise and we're not too keen on the word 'fix' as that suggests there's something wrong with you.

From psychology we know that how long it takes to change will depend on where we're at and what we want to change. So what we need to focus on is becoming competent and building up our accomplishments. We know that coaches, whether they are acting coaches or life coaches, succeed in helping people make changes and that these changes are based on developing practical skills. And we know for sure from science that our brains are not fixed and change is possible. We hope this is reassuring news for you, as we move on to different types of confidence and what type of confidence you aspire to having.

ASK YOURSELF

Q Which area in your life would you most like to develop confidence?

Q Right now, what are you learning to do?

Q Is it really lack of confidence you need to deal with or resistance to changing?

Q Are you lacking in confidence – or stuck in a rut? If you can reframe lack of confidence in something as being stuck in a rut, how can you tackle this? Can you change your routine and usual habits to help you develop confidence?

Q What course can you enrol on now?

CHAPTER 8

WHAT TYPE OF CONFIDENCE DO YOU ASPIRE TO?

I f we had asked you this question at the very beginning, you may have been baffled and answered 'any confidence will do'. So far, we've aimed to give you an understanding of real confidence being a state of mind that:

- Comes from within.
- Is genuine.
- Feels calm and excited at the same time, and above all:
- Is true to your inherent nature and all your hopes and dreams.

In Part 1 we examined how confident you are, and in Part 2 we helped you analyse why you lack confidence. In Part 3 we're showing you how to learn to be confident, and in Chapter 7 we kicked off by explaining that yes, confidence is a skill that you can learn. Along the way we've given you lots of confidence boosters, simple everyday tips that enhance your confidence without you making any radical changes. We're hoping that by now you're already feeling more positive and that your confidence is emerging.

This is the point where we want to raise the question of what type of confidence you aspire to. We want to help you ensure that you're clear about what real confidence means for you. One of the problems with lack of confidence is not being able to judge confidence in others. Just as serious financial problems make people feel being a multimillionaire would bring happiness, it's the same with chronic lack of confidence. Perhaps you are envious of other people's ample confidence and compare yourself constantly. Or maybe you have a sibling or close friend who is the outwardly confident one and feel you're constantly being compared.

By exploring confidence in different countries and cultures, as well as analysing different types of confidence, you will gain a deeper understanding that the world doesn't divide into those who do (have confidence) and people like you who feel they don't. You'll discover as you begin to observe confidence that it's not just in black and white, confidence comes in all sorts of colours and shades. This will give you a clearer idea of how real confidence might fit for you.

FOLLOW PEOPLE WHO TRULY INSPIRE YOU ON SOCIAL MEDIA

Surprisingly, one 2008 study[1] found that people with low self-esteem who follow celebrities can feel better about themselves. These 'parasocial' relationships can have beneficial effects because they help people feel closer to their ideal selves. Bearing this study in mind, think about how your favourite celebrities reflect your ideal self. Search for figures (like your favourite authors, or comedians) who are not part of controlled Hollywood perfection and are not selling a perfect lifestyle. Are there people who offer inspiration and boost your mind so that you can use social media to *empower* your mind? Following people in the public eye who are informative, campaign for a better society and planet, offer lots of inspiring quotes and share about themselves in a real way can help you become your ideal real you. They act as good role models, and when you have an off day they can help get you back on track.

CONFIDENCE AROUND THE WORLD

One fun way to understand confidence is to study it wherever you travel to. It makes people-watching even more interesting. Go to any major city in the world and the same smartphones, fashion brands and coffee chains are there. We watch HBO and Scandinavian dramas, read the Huffington Post and debate Apple versus PC. But how do our notions of confidence compare worldwide? How does where you live affect the way you view your confidence? Awareness of other cultures can help you understand confidence on a deeper level. It can help you decide what kind of confidence you aspire to.

Academic studies don't often take cultural variations into account, which makes international experts like psychologists Dr Tomas

Chamorro-Premuzic and Dr Ilona Boniwell all the more interesting and valuable. Given that there are cultural variations to psychological traits, the studies that matter most are either international or based on our own culture. Boniwell points to Asian nations scoring lower in self-esteem studies than Anglo-Saxons, because it's not socially acceptable in Asian nations to focus on oneself. Similarly Russians score lower in happiness studies compared to the British or Americans, because it's not socially acceptable to brag about happiness.

> **" Many studies are made in the US and are applicable to the American population. So we cannot take all discoveries as absolute and universal. "**
>
> Dr Ilona Boniwell, positive psychologist

In any case, there is only a certain amount we can learn from academic studies. Our own observations are also important in our development. Even for psychologists, it's their own experience and observations that can inspire their research.

As an Argentine who migrated to the UK in 1998 and has divided his time between the US and UK for the past 15 years, Chamorro-Premuzic is acutely aware of cultural variations in confidence. Indeed his fascination with confidence began in his home country as he realized that national over-confidence did not tally with the reality of Argentina's government and economy. This is what led to the big question in his mind: what's the point of confidence without actual competence?

In the UK, Chamorro-Premuzic discovered a much more complex culture of self-deprecation and faking modesty. Then in the US he found an attitude based on confidence being within easy reach, but with little emphasis on developing competence, which 'is anti-intellectual and misinformed'.

He finds the Mediterraneans over-confident and describes Northern Europeans as more focused on competence. Most fascinating to him, culturally, are the North East Asians who are not only under-confident, but culturally favour humility. 'In Asia you are supposed to see yourself as more humble than you are,' he says. 'You are almost embarrassed about compliments, and you're much more favourably pre-disposed to take on board negative feedback.'

Moving to France after living in the UK for 15 years from the age of 20 has been fascinating for Boniwell. While in the UK we're currently pursuing confidence, in France they have a veneer of confidence. She explains that the education system in France is hyper critical and doesn't instill real confidence in people. It's worth remembering this next time you're in Paris. Is that Parisian frostiness confidence, arrogance or even rudeness?

Growing up in Latvia and Russia meant Boniwell experienced the Germanic–Nordic type of quiet confidence, though she left Russia before the huge cultural change post-Soviet-Union when a high degree of outward confidence became the new norm. 'The culture is competitive and you are expected to constantly position your importance.'

"The question is: which confidence are we striving for?"

Dr Ilona Boniwell, positive psychologist

NICE, OR ULTIMATE, CONFIDENCE?

Observing and discussing cultural attitudes to confidence is inspiring for the questions and discussions that arise. Boniwell points to Nordic countries as examples of 'nice' confidence, citing Iceland, where she was recently teaching, as a culture of remarkable confidence. 'There was an all-round nice confidence. It's a country of astonishingly confident women. They look calm and engaged, happy in their bodies and clothes, without trying hard to look sexy. There is amazing balance between work and family as most work finishes at 4pm and men and women share looking after children equally. There is a feeling of pride in the country and culture. It's not a show-off confidence; it's a profound one.'

DR NATASHA BULDEO ON THE RISKS OF ULTIMATE CONFIDENCE

If you're a workaholic wondering why there's no correlation between the hours you work and your self-esteem, it might be that your idea of confidence is an extreme one in the sense that you are surrendering too much of yourself in the hope of achieving ultimate confidence. Buldeo says Japanese Samurai Warriors exemplify ultimate confidence because they were trained to 'do or die', in other words they were so confident that they accepted death. As an expert in physiology, Buldeo explains that acceptance of any situation has an impact on the body and mind. 'You go into battle – whether a metaphorical battle or a real battle – in a relaxed state. You face whatever you need to face. You give it your best shot.'

But there's a flip side to this, namely the repercussions in modern Japanese society that include high levels of suicide. 'Culturally the give-it-all-or-die mentality lingers on in the zeitgeist,' says Buldeo. 'This type of confidence becomes if I'm not succeeding at giving it my all then it's not worth living.'

Lack of anything tends to create a fantasy of replenishing that gap with a surplus. Just as lack of money or time makes a human being fantasize about winning the lottery or never having to go to work, lack of confidence might be making you wish you had more than ample confidence. If in your mind you feel that more than ample confidence is an unhealthy ultimate confidence (where in fact you are pushing yourself too much), then this won't nurture you. Nice confidence, on the other hand, is not only more attainable, it's also sustainable. When confidence is real it works in synergy with all of you. Remember that confidence is based on knowing yourself and that will at times mean identifying that there's something you don't know how to do or don't feel comfortable doing. Rather than pushing yourself to limits you'll be looking for balance.

IS OVER-CONFIDENCE REWARDED?

As you start to observe and analyse confidence you'll inevitably start to question over-confident types. You might admire your colleague who manages to bluff his way through any situation to the extent that he covers up major errors at work; but if someone is covering up their incompetence, then where does the confidence come from? You may be thinking 'but what does it matter if over-confidence pays off?' And you're right, it does pay off. A 2011 study by the University of Edinburgh and the University of California, San Diego,[2] showed that over-confidence pays off in high-risk situations. However, it can also backfire, with the authors citing the 2008 financial crash and the 2003 war in Iraq as examples.

> **Over-confidence is arrogance. Arrogance is unmerited confidence. There's an inflated ego and misjudgment of personal value and abilities.**
>
> Annie Ashdown, confidence coach

Still, these major international events may seem far removed from daily, normal life. How about social media where over-confidence reigns? While the internet and social media are still new areas when it comes to research, what's emerging will be comforting if you feel uncomfortable in the virtual world. A 2015 study by psychologists at Brunel University,[3] London, found that Facebook users who scored high on narcissism as a personality trait updated their status more frequently, and that they were motivated by a need for attention and validation. The study also found that people with low self-esteem posted updates about their romantic partner more frequently.

A 2011 study published in the journal *Cyberpsychology, Behavior and Social Networking*[4] found that women who base their self-worth on appearance share more photos and have larger networks on social media. The results are hardly surprising news, but for anyone lacking in confidence about their looks it may be reassuring to have confirmation that this activity is based on a need for attention rather than a sign of inner confidence. It could be an indication of a type of over-confidence based on appearances, but as it's not inward, some may not distinguish this as 'real' confidence. One interesting detail of the study's findings was that participants whose self-worth was based on academic competence, family love and support and being a good person spent less time online.

We all know at least one person whose Facebook or Twitter profiles boost their confidence because of the numbers of likes, followers, shares, favourites they receive. Researchers at the University of Pittsburgh and Columbia Business School,[5] writing in the *Journal of Consumer Research* in 2013, warned against behaving according to high levels of Facebook likes and positive comments. The study found that self-esteem fuelled by social media can lead to credit-card debt, higher alcohol and sugar consumption and other poor self-control behaviours.

You might believe that over-confident people are rewarded by society, and suspect that we're going to tell you this is a negative belief. Unfortunately, they are; and there is scientific proof of this. A 2012 study at IESE Business School, University of Navarra,[6] published in the *Journal of Personality and Social Psychology,* confirmed that over-confidence helped people achieve social status. Incompetent and over-confident people are promoted, and because they gain more status and prestige they are admired. The authors of the study do warn that organizations should *not* pay attention to self-rated confidence but should evaluate competence. Another crucial and depressing detail in the study is that group members did not think of their high-status peers as over-confident, but viewed them as terrific.

What's evident so far is that over-confidence is not desirable or attractive. We hope you'll start identifying over-confident people and asking yourself: what is the result of their over-confidence? How does their over-confidence have an impact on others? Aspiring to this type of confidence will not help you on a real level. In any case it's unlikely that you would be able to achieve what essentially is arrogance. (The fact that you are reading this book shows that you have the emotional intelligence to help and develop yourself, so we know you are not arrogant!).

NARCISSISM ISN'T CONFIDENCE

Though we've focused more on confidence being based on mastering new situations and taking actions to do so, an element of confidence does come from how we view and assess ourselves. On the surface self-esteem is about how positive we feel about ourselves. Only it's more complicated.

The classic definition of self-esteem came from one of the first teachers of psychology, philosopher and psychologist William James[7] in 1890. He believed it's the ratio between our successes and goals. It's worth noting that success to James was our *perception* of achieving these goals.

Psychologists now divide self-esteem into authentic and defensive, positive and negative, competent and incompetent, worthy and unworthy. One 2008 study by Michael Kernis at the University of Georgia[8] found a further difference between secure and fragile self-esteem. Individuals with fragile high self-esteem can come across as aggressive, defensive and unlikeable.

> " Self-esteem can be defensive and narcissistic, based on no competence. This self-esteem is not good. It's puffed up, unstable, and unpleasant to other people. "

Dr Ilona Boniwell, positive psychologist

Chamorro-Premuzic, in his book *Confidence: The Surprising Truth About How Much You Need and How to Get It* (Profile, 2013), cites several studies that demonstrate a correlation between narcissism and over-confidence. One study, by Detroy Paulhaus at the University of British Columbia[9] on self-deception, tested anonymous participants with a self-reported general knowledge quiz in which participants had to state how much knowledge they had about various topics. Participants were also assessed on narcissism and how they present information about themselves. The results showed that people who *claimed* they knew more despite not actually knowing more were more narcissistic. From a low-confidence vantage point it can be tempting to assume that over-confident people have the chutzpah to lie to those around them, when in fact all the studies show is that they are lying to themselves.

BECOME A GOOD CONFIDENCE JUDGE

Becoming a good confidence judge will help you be gentler with yourself. You'll be able to focus on your abilities and what you enjoy *doing*. Next time someone tells you they are great at something, ask yourself how you can be sure of this. Is the friend who claims to be good at technology but doesn't know the answer to your techno-question confident at claiming to be confident? Start paying attention to people around you who are doing things they love and who are clearly knowledgeable, but don't label themselves as amazing or confident: that friend who has a passion for baking bread; the friend who is at the allotment in all weather; the colleague who always manages to sort out annoying technical issues; the neighbour who complains effectively to the council.

DR TOMAS CHAMORRO-PREMUZIC ON DEALING WITH OVER-CONFIDENCE

As an Argentine, Chamorro-Premuzic has more than an academic interest in this subject. He experienced individual and collective over-confidence leading to self-destruction when the economy in his country collapsed in 1998. If over-confidence can lead to self-destruction, does that mean over-confident people change their ways?

'It is always harder to adjust to failure when you are used to success. But the point still holds: the healthy and adaptive reaction is to have a reality check and lower your confidence. For instance, in the financial crisis some people will have noticed they are not as rich as they actually are, accepted it, and dealt with it starting from scratch (much like Japan and Germany did after the shock of losing the Second World War). Others may stay deluded or blame someone else, meaning they are more confident but less competent.'

When it comes to public speaking and presentations, Chamorro-Premuzic himself admits he was over-confident in the past. He'd 'wing it' in lectures early on in his career when he thought it was more important to entertain the students and be popular. As someone with self-awareness, he gradually changed because he wanted to be effective. 'There are two scenarios, an audience who know you're talking rubbish or a naïve audience who will fall for a charming charlatan.'

Too much confidence blocks people from becoming their best selves because they have no incentive to gain true competence.

'They think they're great. Low-confident people on the other hand have every incentive to close the gap between their ideal self (the person they want to be) and their perceived actual self (the person they think they are).'

DR NITASHA BULDEO ON THE STRESS OF BEING OVER-CONFIDENT

'The whole thing with over-confidence is that a person gets away with something once, gets away with it again, it becomes a formula. That's why forgiveness with reason is a good thing – but it can also enable people to get away with detrimental actions and repeat them. When confidence is based on a formula of getting away with it, there is always the fear of being found out. Over-confident people experience severely increased heart rate, hyper tension and stress. There tends to be a negative spiral. They need to feel up-up-up and aren't aware of the body expressing anxiety. That's why you see the downward spiral with a lot of celebrities. It's confidence that needs to be fed. However, they often don't pay attention to what's going on internally. How do they cope with the stresses that celebrity brings – they drink and do drugs to dull the senses. A lot of people overuse prescription drugs, or their hyper-sensitized state becomes chronic pain.'

REAL PEOPLE

"I thought I was jealous because I lacked confidence"

– Lorraine

Lorraine found herself constantly upset by a 'yummy mummy' on the committee organizing charity events for her sons' school. This coincided with a period of feeling very down about herself. 'I'd lost all confidence in myself on every level. I looked 10 years older than 42 and felt 102. I found it hard to deal with my two (very naughty) boys, and felt knocked back from not being able to get part-time work to keep my brain going. And here was this yummy mummy constantly showing us her perfect Cath Kidston life, posting selfies on Facebook several times a day. Twice a day when I saw her at the school gates I just felt these pangs of something. When we had committee meetings she talked rubbish non-stop, while I'd worked for a charity raising money and I couldn't get a word out. My husband couldn't understand why I was in such a state.'

Most of all Lorraine was wound up with having to deal with her fellow committee member's outright lies in failing to carry out her own duties whilst trying to shift blame onto Lorraine.

'I took it personally. I felt she must think I'm so stupid or so in awe of her. Confronting her was impossible. She accused anyone who dared say anything of being jealous of her looks, figure, home, lifestyle, relationship. I thought I must have been jealous because I lacked confidence. It really never occurred to me that she was lying to herself until something trivial happened. She claimed she hadn't received a crucial email from me – and yet she had replied to it and cc'd all of us on the committee. It was actually very funny. I did feel stupid that I'd been giving myself such a hard time.'

As soon as we start to think about different types of confidence it's not long before we get to over-confidence and narcissism. By people-watching when travelling you can acquire some interesting cultural examples of confidence that can prompt how you develop confidence for yourself. Perhaps your humble guide on the other side of the globe might inspire you by being able to calmly deal with a dangerous animal. Maybe the designer-clad Parisian who corrects your French yet speaks atrocious English might now make you laugh.

As we've seen in this chapter, there is ample international academic research demonstrating how over-confidence can also mean incompetence. Admiring over-confident people can damage your confidence because you yourself overlook your abilities, and by admiring incompetent people you allow others (like your employer) to overlook your own skills. Because your competence is overlooked you then get into a cycle of not being able to find confidence from within. We also live in a narcissistic society which doesn't help you, so it's important to be aware of how you respond to narcissists. Now that you are aware that narcissism isn't confidence, we hope you won't admire and respond to people who use the fact that people like you admire them to feel great. This not only undermines your confidence, it's an unhealthy role model for confidence and is also damaging to our society.

We hope that the kind of confidence you want to develop for yourself will be based on feeling good about developing your abilities to your maximum potential. Confidence doesn't mean you have to be a loud show-off, so if you've had any resistance because this just isn't you, you know now that confidence can be quiet.

ASK YOURSELF

Q Can you tell the difference between real confidence and bravado?

Q When you visualize a confident you, how will you feel inside and how will you come across in person?

Q Who do you know who personifies the type of confidence you aspire to? Why?

Q Who do you know who claims to be confident but is incompetent?

Q Which celebrities or public figures represent the type of confidence you would like to develop for yourself?

CHAPTER 9

CONFIDENCE-BUILDING HABITS

A s soon as you think of confidence as something you should work on every day rather than an abstract goal post, you'll become aware of a major attitude change. You'll be focused on the ongoing process. We believe that creating a series of habits that build our confidence is the key to real confidence. If you wait for the moment when you need to be confident to practise what you've learnt, it's too late. In this chapter you will learn how habits that appear to have nothing to do with confidence help you develop confidence organically.

There are 15 habits and we suggest you work your way through them, moving on to the next one when the habit becomes second nature and you don't even have to think about it. Some habits may take no time whatsoever, and others will require more awareness. There's no need to get bogged down though. If you find that one of these is particularly difficult for you, move on to the next one, and come back to it later. The more confidence-building habits you acquire, the quicker it will be to learn new ones.

1. ASSESS YOURSELF

Instead of staying in the fogginess that is lack of confidence, take a stock check. Forget *needing* confidence, what is it you *want* and/or *need* to do? Every time you feel wobbly and sense you are falling into 'I'm hopeless, I can't do this' territory, stop, detach yourself from your emotions and analyse where you're at, where you need to get to, and what you need to learn. Keep assessing yourself. Remember: this isn't about being critical of yourself, but simply identifying what you need to learn. You want to leave the drudge of being an employee and set up your own business but it seems impossible? Assess where you need to get to, and what you need to get there – and keep assessing. Do you need to take an accounting course? Do you need to save money to have a cushion? Do you need to downsize to help you invest in your idea? Do you need to network with people who can help you? 'The goal must become competence in what matters to you,' says Tomas Chamorro-Premuzic. 'Start with an accurate assessment of yourself, and ask yourself: how much do I need to work at this?'

2. KEEP LEARNING

> **"There is a bias towards thinking of confidence as generic. To improve your confidence it's much easier to work at a specific level. "**
>
> Dr Tomas Chamorro-Premuzic, Psychologist and Professor of Business Psychology at UCL

If you are always taking a course in something, you are developing a six-pack confident brain. Regardless of what you want to become confident at, any learning has a spin-off effect. Instead of dwelling on lack of confidence at work, for example, take courses in anything that interests you outside work. The combination of pursuing a passion and engaging your brain in learning will give you a happier energy, and your confidence will spill out at work.

Let's take a look at research in 2012 at the University of Melbourne,[1] which concluded that there's a strong correlation between confidence and success at work. Of course this is stating the obvious, until we look at what the study really looked at: that those reporting high confidence from early school throughout their education and right through to the present day were more successful. Although the media presented this as a reason to fake it until you make it, what the study really highlights is something entirely different: education provides a solid foundation to confidence.

As adults, regardless of where we got to academically, there's nothing to stop us zooming in on specific areas where we need to focus on learning. Since competence leads to confidence, one of the most important habits for boosting your confidence is learning. If you can identify, for example, that learning about new technology would help you at work, then you can find a course at an adult education centre or online.

3. DEVELOP YOUR WILLPOWER

66 Ultimately willpower trumps everything: if you want something badly, you will try to get it, regardless of how you rate your skills. 99

Dr Tomas Chamorro-Premuzic, Psychologist and Professor of Business Psychology at UCL

You may wonder about the curious paradox of that person who you know lacks confidence and yet is able to somehow achieve their goals. The answer is willpower. Rather than focusing on not having confidence, switch your thinking to how much you want something, why you want it, and what will happen when you get this. As soon as you focus on willpower, what will happen is that you'll identify what gets in the way. Let's say you don't have the confidence to go running, but really want to run a marathon to raise money for a charity that has helped a loved one deal with a terrible disease. It's focusing on your motivation that will give you the willpower to start running and slowly achieve the marathon.

4. TALK ABOUT YOUR POSITIVE EXPERIENCES

66 People dwell too much on failures rather than successes. Given that it is the successes that are the building bricks to confidence, talking about

these and understanding what happened is important. 🙶

Dr Ilona Boniwell, positive psychologist

Do you spend more time talking about how you made a mess of things and what you can't do? Consider this from now on a bad habit and switch to talking about something, anything, that was even a tiny achievement. Rather than going over and over how rubbish you are in one or every area of your life, talking about the process of trying and making small progress is a habit that will help you make greater progress. Dr Ilona Boniwell refers to research in psychology known as 'active constructive responding', which in a nutshell means focusing on our positive rather than negative experiences. The studies in this area of research have found that couples who discuss what has kept them together and what is good about their relationship are the couples who stay longer together, rather than those who talk about the problems in their relationship. Adapting this principle to areas where you are striving to develop confidence will help you enormously. Let's say you go to pieces in job interviews but you are getting lots of interviews. Look for what went well in each one. Maybe this time you managed not to go blank, maybe you succeeded at smiling, maybe you remembered what you're great at. Don't even discuss what went wrong.

5. TONE DOWN YOUR WORST THOUGHTS

Being real in any area in our lives begins with self-awareness and we've kicked off this section with recommending that you develop the habit of assessing yourself. We're also aware that being real means accepting how you feel. So if you feel terrible and your thoughts are terrible, that's where you're at. You don't have to stay there though. In order to shift you just need to get into the habit of toning down your worst thoughts. 'I'm going to be a disaster when I pitch for business and then I'll get the sack', can be toned down to 'I'm not going to be brilliant, but my boss knows this is my first time and will make allowances'.

The basis of cognitive behavioural therapy is identifying the thought and then working out if there is evidence that this is correct (has your boss told you will be sacked if your presentation is rubbish; if you've never presented before what evidence is there that you will be rubbish?).

Modifying your thoughts is way more manageable than a complete radical change. 'It's about questioning whether our thinking is correct so that we get to the explanation that we may be *partly* right and *partly* wrong,' says Boniwell. 'For example if you are anxious, it's true that you don't know the future, so things may go wrong; but perhaps you can get to a half way sense that it's not going to be *so* bad.'

6. DITCH THINKING FOR DOING

66The antidote for worrying and obsessing is DOING. 99

Niki Flacks, acting coach, psychologist, therapist

We're not going to pretend that anyone's state of mind and how they feel about themselves is going to change overnight or even within days. Bearing in mind what we've said earlier, that confidence fluctuates and is affected by several factors, we know you'll have wobbly moments or even days. This is when you need to get out of your head. As soon as you become aware of too much thinking, start *doing* anything. Absolutely any activity can help ignite confidence.

As a therapist, Niki Flacks encourages her clients to be practical in order to get away from that inner critical voice telling you negative things. Flacks describes how yogis developed challenging poses because they had trouble meditating when sitting still: 'Yoga is a moving meditation. You're not trying to wrap your brain around something. Your brain is peaceful because your body is doing the work.' So next time you start to feel yourself worrying about your career, for example, go for a brisk walk, clean the house, or do some gardening instead.

7. ADOPT GOOD POSTURE

It's not surprising that a 2009 study at Ohio University[2] found that people told to sit up straight felt better at what they were doing and were viewed as better than participants slumped over their desk. Posture is one of those things, however, that we tend to forget when we're self-absorbed. Yet what we do with our bodies changes the chemistry in our brains and there is ample science to back this up. Some of the most recent groundbreaking studies have been led by social psychologist Professor Amy Cuddy at Harvard Business School.[3] What Cuddy and her colleagues have found is that power poses (opening up our bodies rather than closing them down) change our hormones so we are less reactive to stress and more fired up with testosterone energy. This isn't just about how others see us, but more crucially about how we feel. Just two minutes of opening up and stretching out our arms (instead of sitting huddled up) *before* a job interview zaps tension and boosts confidence.

Rather than randomly trying to nervously change your posture *during* a stressful situation, and then feeling it's weird and fake, develop the habit of becoming aware of your posture on a daily basis. Make a mental note to open up your body (even when you're alone) as this shifts your mind towards becoming more confident. Remember that Cuddy's findings confirm that just two minutes alters the brain chemistry, so if you can practise this for just two minutes a day, that's a powerful habit.

8. EAT A WELL-BALANCED DIET

It may seem obvious to reiterate that you have to eat healthily, but you may have a sneaky question about whether it's really connected to confidence. You may be aware that when you're stressed and worried, there are times when you reach for more coffee, or overeat or forget to eat, even if you're normally a healthy eater. These are in fact the times when you really need to pay attention to good nutrition and get into the habit of zapping the bad habits. The extra coffee/sugar/alcohol when you're on holiday, relaxed, feeling good is fine. But when you're working on developing confidence these can derail you and you'll find yourself off course.

9. EXERCISE

❝Exercise helps build endurance in the mind for dealing with everyday life and day to day problems.❞

Dr Nitasha Buldeo, research scientist

Now you may associate exercise with losing weight, and you may insist that you are just not a gym person. But if you make some form of exercise – and it doesn't have to involve the gym – part of your routine, the mental effects will be huge. (And, sure, your body will benefit too.) Finding some sort of physical activity you love is essential because when our bodies move the brain releases feel-good endorphins. Could you cycle to work? Is there a local ramblers group you might join for weekend walks? How about that ballroom dancing ad that jumps out at you? Can you transform that silent rage you feel at work into kick-boxing energy?

Exercise does more for the mind than just help us to feel good. It also strengthens the mind and makes it more resilient, so that you can feed the strength and resilience into a specific area you are looking to gain confidence in. It's not just athletes who need to build endurance to compete.

10. FIVE MINUTE MORNING WIGGLE

If that heading was meditation (or mindfulness) you might have skipped it on the basis of having tried it but not being able to 'do it'. Buldeo believes that reconnecting to the body helps our mind find solutions to problems, and following this short exercise every morning can set you up for the day:

'Lie down and focus on your body, starting with wriggling your toes and working your way up and through the body, becoming aware of it. You need to wiggle or move each body area as this focuses attention on that area and makes you more aware of it. When you get to your head, if you have a thought, then just let it go. The entire body remembers. We have muscle memory, and every cell has DNA, so every bit of our body remembers. It's not all in the head. Feeling confident is about using your entire body. When you feel grounded you feel true to yourself, so use the entire body.'

11. BREATHE, BREATHE, BREATHE

It's the simplest thing, we do it without thinking, and yet cultivating the habit of breathing properly can totally transform the mind without having to do anything else. What tends to happen when we're stressed or feeling bad about ourselves or rushing around trying to do too much is that we breathe in a shallow way. It's easy not to notice this, which is why getting into the habit of tuning in to how we are breathing is important. Always remember that real confidence is about feeling calm, and when we're calm our heart rate is normal. The fastest way to become calm is to breathe properly.

Understanding the science behind breathing will help you remember to breathe. The brain needs oxygen and deep breathing oxygenates the brain. This process then sparks off a series of physiological reactions: blood is pumped to the organs so they can do their work, which includes adjusting our heart rate.

If we're feeling negative about ourselves, Buldeo suggests a breathing technique that will immediately elevate your mood: inhale deeply and exhale rapidly, a technique known in yoga as breath of fire.

If somebody knocks you off balance and you feel wobbly, Buldeo recommends the alternating nostrils technique which circulates the breath: inhale from one nostril using your fingers to close the other, swap the fingers to exhale and inhale and continue. She suggests starting with the nostril on the side of your dominant hand, so right for right-handed people.

To counter nerves, Buldeo suggests the Japanese Hara technique (used in Japanese martial arts): stand with your feet shoulder-width apart, put your right hand about the navel, breathe deep from your nose so you feel the breath enter the entire area of your belly, then breathe out through your nose.

Exhaling through the mouth is faster because the mouth is a larger area. When we use the nostrils the breathing is slower, which is ideal for any situation where you're feeling anxious or nervous.

12. TAKE GOOD CARE OF YOURSELF

❝You cannot have self-confidence without self-care. To feel confidence, top up your energy supply. What energizes you?❞

Dawn Breslin, confidence coach

When you don't have confidence, one common mistake is to believe that it's possible to just 'have' it. You will have absorbed by now from reading this book that this isn't the case. Instead we need to always think in terms of trying new things and learning and feeling better as we get better at something. But to do this we do need to start from really looking after ourselves. You may be tempted when you feel lacking in confidence to look at confident high flyers and wonder why you can't be like them, but perhaps you also know some confident high flyers who burnt out and lost their confidence because they weren't looking after themselves.

Looking after yourself every day and at all times when you don't have confidence is a habit that feeds you confidence. Looking after yourself means eating well and exercising, sleeping and resting – and much more.

When you need confidence to make changes, looking after yourself is a crucial starting point. 'Change takes energy,' says Breslin 'and you need energy to feel strong.' To prepare for change you need to be present and stop worrying about how lack of confidence is stopping you from sorting out your future or how it has messed up your past.

Breslin advises making a set of daily rituals and popping the list on your dressing table or above your kettle. Her own routine is to put on a favourite playlist every morning, load the washing machine and clean the kitchen. She takes breaks during the day just to be with herself over a cup of tea and at the end of the day she always goes to 'her' beach. 'I've set my life up so I can walk out and be seduced by the energy around me.'

13. TURN YOUR HOME INTO YOUR HAVEN

By the time you have finished this book, you might have booked at least one new course to do, and your attention will be on developing skills step by step in any activity or area where you'd like confidence. Whether there's just one thing you want to conquer or whether you want to get back to your former confident self or find the reserves to follow a dream, you do need a solid base. And that's none other than home. If home is a mess and you don't feel good at home making even a small change will be harder. Home is our support camp for a long life journey.

'If someone were to climb Everest there are base camps along the route, and inside those base camps there is everything you need to re-energize to climb the mountain,' says Breslin. 'Life is like climbing Everest. It's hard and it's exhausting. So what's in your base camp? How do you actively replenish your energy? In order to thrive we must learn to prioritze slowing down and finding balance. We must make a connection with our energy and learn how to manage it: is it depleted or full? If depleted how can I top up? Your home is one of your base camps – does it nurture, hold or energize you?'

Make sure you have a simple routine for cleaning and tidying your home, and line up a support system for fixing anything that's broken. Declutter and fill your space with things that you love. Set out to make your home as beautiful as you can so that when you arrive you step into your own positive energy, and when you leave you're leaving having been supported by this energy. By tidy we don't mean that you have to go against your natural tendency to not order everything perfectly, it's possible to be 'creatively' tidy for sure. But if it's untidiness that brings you down and wastes your time then sort out immediately. If you're trying to conquer fear of public speaking, for example, and you can't even find your notes for your presentation, that's not going to help. If you're unhappy with house mates or neighbours, do consider moving or finding ways to change your situation.

14. SUPPORT DON'T COMPETE

If you are working in a competitive environment you may feel that there's nothing you can do, but in fact becoming supportive to those around you will help you because you will actively be changing the competitive culture. Just because an environment isn't nurturing doesn't mean you have to go along with not being nurturing. If you find that you get sucked in to gossiping about co-workers and being critical, this undermines your own confidence. Comparing and competing does nothing to fuel confidence.

We're not saying that you should make fake compliments – we want to encourage you to be real. Observe your co-workers more (instead of worrying about yourself). If you notice that somebody timid manages to stand up to the office bully even in a small way, then let that person know you noticed and admired this. Resist joining in with any gossip or judgemental comments about anyone. If someone is stressed make a gesture that helps them, whether it's making them a cup of tea or making them laugh.

'Ingrained in every career is ambition, so people end up endlessly comparing and competing,' says Flacks, who visits many types of corporations to train people as well running acting workshops. 'If we learn to encourage each other we feel better about ourselves. It doesn't have to be dog eats dog. What I've seen is that people totally change in a work environment when there is support. They glow. They start to feel good about themselves.'

15. BE WITH CONFIDENT PEOPLE

66 If we equate confidence with being authentic, then we attract authentic people. 99

Annie Ashdown, confidence coach

How confident are your friends – really? Are you surrounded by insecure people? Who in your circle is working on themselves, reading books like this or seeing a therapist or taking courses in new subjects? Do you secretly feel that some of your friends can be fake in certain situations? If you are avoiding certain people because you feel insecure and don't feel good enough – confident enough – to be around them, well now is the time to change that. Follow confidence! Be around confident people. Cultivate the company of confident people. In the confidence robbers section, we highlighted that negative people diminish your confidence. Avoiding them is a start, and seeking out positive, confident people is an ongoing process. This isn't about ditching anyone (unless they undermine you) but about drawing new people to you.

***

We hope you agree that these 15 habits are very simple to implement. We know that waiting to take a big action is challenging for most people because it's scary to get started, so that's why we recommend little daily changes. It may be tempting to make several little changes, but that can be equally overwhelming and the result can be counterproductive. You may be developing other habits to fuel confidence in a specific area, as well as trying to follow through these habits and the other advice in the book. If you sense it's becoming too much, then step back. Focus on one habit at a time until it becomes routine, and then move on to the next one.

ASK YOURSELF

Q What daily habits do you currently have that help you feel confident?

Q What daily habits can you admit make you feel bad about yourself?

Q Which new habit would make the most difference to your confidence?

Q Are you surrounded by people with good, confidence-boosting habits? Who are they? What can you learn from them?

Q What can you *do* that will help you develop the habit of thinking positively and confidently?

CHAPTER 10

KEEPING TRACK OF YOUR CONFIDENCE EVERY DAY

When you bought this book you may have had a set idea of what confidence is and no doubt knew that so far nothing you've tried has worked. Our experts have all, from their different perspectives, agreed that real confidence comes from within and isn't superficial. By now, hopefully you will be motivated to focus on gaining knowledge, expertise and skills that will give you the foundation to feel confident. And ideally you will be inspired to think in terms of trying and celebrating little achievements so that step by step you feel able to conquer any situation. By giving you a sense of how different types of confidence feel in the body you will be aware of what to look out for. You know now that if your heart is pounding and you've had too much to drink this certainly isn't confidence, but if you're feeling calm and comfortable in a situation with a little nervy twinge of excitement that this is.

We've encouraged you to reflect on confidence in relation to who you are throughout the book through the tests and the Ask Yourself questions. You'll have an understanding now of why you lack confidence and which factors in your life have affected you, so that you won't be blaming yourself for being inadequate and so that you can look back at external circumstances like critical teachers or employers knowing it was circumstances rather than a fault within you that has affected your confidence. We've outlined confidence robbers in detail so that you can arm yourself with the necessary inner armour to avoid these.

Though certainly some people are born with a confidence gene, all of our formidable experts have shown that confidence is a skill that can be learnt. By encouraging you to think about the type of confidence you aspire to we're urging you to be true to yourself. If you are a larger than life type of person we don't want you to feel that you must express your confidence in a larger than life way, in other words we're saying don't feel you have to advertise it: show, don't tell. And if you're quiet and reflective we don't want you to change that because we don't believe that there is a correlation between confidence and loudness.

Throughout this book we've given you confidence boosters in the form of very simple pieces of advice that may not even appear to be directly connected to confidence, yet strengthen your inner foundation. And in the last chapter we gave you a series of confidence building habits so that you can recalibrate your approach. As these habits become second nature, you will organically feel confident.

In this section, we thought we'd get down to some basics, namely daily life. What we're aware of is that it's possible to embark on developing habits and making plans to conquer this and that, and having light bulb moments of what and who affects confidence levels, yet at the same time overlooking some very basic obstacles. We could give you the perfect recipe for, let's say, a Thai curry. We could tell you where to go to get authentic ingredients from Thai greengrocers, to which supermarkets stock everything you need. We could give you a choice between making the paste yourself from scratch, or the best ones to buy. But if your kitchen is in a mess, you don't really cook anyway, and you don't have the basic equipment, all that advice might be wasted.

This section sets out some basic life scenarios. We discuss routine daily life and family life; we tackle work because that's where most people spend most of their time; we look at social situations, including dating, because human beings inevitably are thrown together; and last but not least we consider body image because we know that how you feel about your looks and body do affect your confidence levels and we're not just going to dismiss this with 'oh, love yourself'. With each section we identify potential traps and show you easy ways to avoid falling into these.

DAILY LIFE

One of the problems with setting out to develop confidence skills in a particular area is that the routine of daily life itself can get in the way. If you're frustrated because you lack confidence about changing jobs or finding a new circle of friends following divorce, or any similar situation, it's as though your mind is consumed by this to the extent that you find it hard to concentrate on being in the moment. There is a danger of withdrawing into yourself and you need to stop this in order to formulate the process of developing skills and trying to accomplish something new. There is a very simple way to break out of this and that's to do something, anything, with others. Become part of something, whether it's signing a petition to stop a supermarket replacing an independent shop, joining a mindfulness group, running a marathon for charity. Make sure it's something that makes you engage with others, however briefly, as opposed to something you just do online. So if you join a human rights group and participate in social media discussions, make sure you also go to a campaigning talk or a demonstration they organize.

When you get so caught up in your head that you can't see what's around you, you lose your personal mojo. Being aware of our society and being part of it is important for us as human beings. Social psychologists have even linked personal self-esteem to society's values. One major global study published by the online *Personality and Social Psychology Bulletin* in 2008 found that we base and define self-esteem on our culture's dominant values. The study at the CLLE[1] (Laboratoire Cognition, Langue, Langages, Ergonomie, CNRS/Université de Toulouse II-Le Mirail) surveyed 16–17 year-olds in 19 countries all over the world.

By stepping out of your head and looking at the issues going on around you, you are not only giving your poor brain a rest from all the battering it gets, but by connecting with your neighbourhood, community, society, you will feel part of something and that will give you a platform to feel more connected to yourself. If there is a local campaign to save a library and you're a big reader, you're reminding yourself of why you love to read and why reading is important. By helping to communicate your passion to others, even by just handing out some leaflets or asking people to sign a petition, you are reinforcing positive messages about yourself and escaping from the cycle of 'oh I'm not good enough, I'm not confident enough'. When that library is saved you'll know you played a part. If you can play a part in saving a library, you can certainly save yourself from feeling bad.

66 Make human connections, because then everything you do matters. 99

Patsy Rodenburg, OBE, voice and leadership coach

Being part of what's around you isn't just about joining something. It's also about being aware of human beings around you in any situation. To get out of being absorbed in chronic lack of confidence getting in your way, start by aiming to make a connection with every person who comes your way. If you lack confidence in dating, saying good morning to the people you pass by in your street every day is a first step towards conquering a fear of meeting strangers. If you hate going to parties, saying something about the weather to the barista when you collect your coffee from the café near work is a step towards making small talk. If you're terrified of making presentations at work, ordering for a family outing at the local pizza place and asking the waiter where he/she is from is a baby step to speaking in front of other people – even if they know you, you've still got to remember what everyone wants. Making connections with others provides confidence fuel.

PATSY RODENBURG ON DEVELOPING YOUR PRESENCE EVERY DAY

'Take time to start and end the day:

- *Sit and breathe low (from the belly) so you set yourself up for a calm day.*
- *Warm up your voice by reading something out loud.*
- *Read out loud to your children at night (or read a poem out loud for yourself).*
- *Make eye contact every day with your partner, your children and the people around you that you love.*

The vast majority of us are born with amazing voices which get closed down. People talk about their natural voice but in fact they mean their habitual voice.

Make connections:

- *Get away from your desk at the office. Make a point of talking to people rather than emailing them.*

- *Make a point of making eye contact and saying hello to people.*
- *Ask for people's names at restaurants or at parties where staff come over with drinks.*
- *Say something to supermarket check-out staff.*
- *Always look around you. Be aware of changes.*

Connect with your body:

- *Walk on the balls of your feet.*
- *Make sure your knees are not locked.*

Be curious:

- *Ask other people questions.*
- *Listen.*

Stay focused:

- *Watch your alcohol consumption. Successful people don't drink excessively.*
- *Speak because what you have to say matters, not just for the sake of speaking.'*

REAL PEOPLE

"My local gym saved me" – Lisa

Lisa became withdrawn when she lost her contract as a graphic designer at the same time as entering a major dispute with her neighbours above her over an illegal extension they made. The combination of being out of work, worrying about money during the recession and a costly legal process made her totally doubt herself. She felt so low she stopped going to her local community gym.

'Pilates and yoga helped me manage chronic back pain, but I couldn't face seeing anyone. My counsellor recommended I pushed myself to go because isolating myself was not doing my confidence any good. She was right. I realized that just being with the regulars who said hello and smiled was a massive support system. The fact that I went and did something with people and managed to smile or almost do the headstand badly or not collapse doing the plank made me remember how to feel good about myself.'

When Lisa's gym was threatened with being taken over and turned into luxury flats, she was surprised to find herself getting passionately involved in the campaign to save it. Instead of her personal problems being so overwhelming that she couldn't take anything else on, because the gym had benefited her so much she was fired up to help. 'I went to council meetings with fellow gym members. I helped get petitions signed in the local area. And we did it: we saved something important in the community. This gave me faith in human nature when I needed it, it stopped me spiralling into negativity. This made me appear confident to my neighbours without trying, so they couldn't bully me and threaten me. In the end they had to back down. I came through that awful period and did find new rewarding work opportunities.'

FAMILY LIFE

Given that the roots of confidence are linked to family, it's no wonder that families trigger confidence crises. Why is it that no matter how many times you set yourself the objective of having a conflict-free conversation with certain family members, it still ends in a disaster? Well, while you may be thinking it's your lack of confidence that's at fault, in fact this is an entirely normal situation for most people. If you can just accept that's how it is, and maybe even try and have a sense of humour about it, you will feel better.

It's all too easy to be self-focused and stuck in the child role even when we are adults. If you can remember to look at your parents as people who themselves may have lacked and still continue to lack confidence, you will feel more compassion towards them. Perhaps your mother is critical because she had a critical mother and has been conditioned to believe this is what parenting is about. Perhaps your father undermines you because he believes in fact he is protecting you from all the worries he secretly suffers. Your brother or sister may be unnecessarily competitive and it may seem childish now that you are adults, but maybe your sibling admires you or envies your choices in life. Who knows. The point is, when a conflict erupts remember it's not about you.

NIKI FLACKS ON HANDLING FAMILY DYNAMICS

'When you are working on yourself, just one conversation with a family member can take you back to square one undoing all the good work you feel you've achieved for yourself. Here is some simple advice from Flacks:

Setting objectives to avoid conflict with family members is pointless because family can press your buttons better than anyone else. Learn to change the subject when the subject gets heated:

* Talk about mutually pleasurable things.
* Laugh. When you're screaming at each other learn to laugh about it.
* Say the words 'I love you' no matter what is going on.'

WORK LIFE

We spend so much of our time at work that it's essential to factor in how this affects our confidence. Spending all day putting on a front, or dealing with a difficult boss or feeling you don't fit in with your co-workers brings up all sorts of feelings even if you're really good at your actual job. All sorts of questions form in your mind about your personality. Why didn't your colleagues ask you to join them for a night out? Why does your less-experienced colleague get all the praise? Why does your immediate boss present your ideas as their ideas? How will you get through the annual Christmas party? With all these daily questions popping into your head, work is where you can risk driving yourself into a no-confidence corner.

If you're working in a grim office environment this can be very destabilizing, so you need to stop yourself from spiralling into low confidence negativity. Life coach Dawn Breslin says this is a situation where you need to inspire and empower your mind before you get to work. One of the best ways to do this is to listen to audio personal development books or meditations on the way to work – and after. If you're allowed headphones at work, find music that helps you. Having a special cup is a symbolic and simple way to connect with yourself. 'Take regular points during the day for a few seconds or minutes to remind you of you, like having a tea in your special cup,' says Breslin.

The big danger in the workplace is that you risk convincing yourself that it's your personality that's flawed and that you have no hope.

As an expert in psychological profiling *and* confidence, Tomas Chamorro-Premuzic is tremendously reassuring. 'Personality only predisposes you to something,' he says. So we are led to believe that extroverts are good at certain jobs like sales, but Chamorro-Premuzic points out that there are plenty of introverts who are successful sales people.

What happens when it comes to work is that advice we receive, starting early on from careers advisors at school and university, is often linked to our personalities. You may have been told you couldn't follow your dream because your personality wasn't the right one. Add to this being told your exam results aren't good enough or you don't have a natural aptitude for a subject, well is it any wonder your confidence was eroded? If you're at the point in your life of giving your dream a go because maybe you've received a lucrative redundancy package, hold onto the fact that you intend to do this rather than doubting yourself because you were once told this dream wasn't right for you. The fact that you are going back to that dream shows it's close to your heart and really is you. Otherwise you'd have forgotten it.

66 If you really want something, negative messages can be overcome. You need a minimum amount of confidence for this. All people need to do is realize that they have been victims of wrong advice. 99

Dr Tomas Chamorro-Premuzic, Psychologist and Professor of Business Psychology at UCL

PATSY RODENBURG ON MANAGING A TEAM CONFIDENTLY

'Introduce formality:

- *When you are a leader there is no such thing as casual. You are on all the time.*
- *Set boundaries. If you're running a team you have to be equal with each person.*
- *Shakespeare says leaders are the Lords and owners of their faces. Remember that.*
- *Confident leadership is clean.*
- *When everyone needs your attention, be formal and gracious.*

Develop empathy:

- *The rational left side of the brain handles data, but it's the empathetic, emotionally intelligent right part of the brain that is the key to confident leadership.*

Exercise your voice:

- *It's very common for new CEOs not to be able to get their voice out. Practise.*

Teach good manners:

- *Young people these days are not taught manners. We have to teach them in a basic and decent way.*
- *Be direct. 'There are no smartphones in this meeting.'*
- *Tell the truth. 'Excuse me. Can you please put your smartphone away and be present.'*
- *Speak sooner rather than later about unacceptable behaviour.*

Be honest like a good parent:

- *Remember actors improve and deliver award-winning performances based on their training to expect and to receive constructive feedback. Give good feedback to produce great work performance (rather than firing people without them even knowing their work wasn't good enough).*
- *Frame feedback in a nurturing environment.*
- *Look at the person and breathe when you tell them the truth. Be present with that person.*

Confidence means staying engaged:

- *With difficult people, avoid going into third-circle energy that comes across as aggressive or introverted first-circle energy that translates as passive aggressive.*
- *Engagement means dialogue. I speak. You listen. You speak. I listen.*
- *Resist trying to control (third-circle energy) or pulling away (first-circle energy).*

Inspiring leaders are profound:

- *Dare to speak to the truth.'*

"I hated getting a promotion"
– Jane

Jane was recently promoted to head of a major IT department when her male boss left for a bigger company. The promotion made the 45-year-old feel extremely anxious even though she had been doing most of the work anyway. 'Even though I did most of the work before I was officially promoted, when I got the official promotion I felt so insecure and lacking in confidence. My husband couldn't understand it. I couldn't sleep. I hated getting a promotion.'

Jane identified that she had two sources of anxiety. The first was going from being one of the team, albeit a senior member, to being in charge and not being everybody's friend. 'I didn't know how to behave. My ex-boss was really matey with everyone, and maybe because he was a bloke that worked. I felt really uneasy from day one. Within a few days people were making comments to me under their breath, like chill out. Fortunately, when I was offered the promotion and gave my reasons for saying no, the HR department said they would send me for management training. I found that really helpful, not just because of the structured advice, but meeting other people on the course who, like me, weren't sure how to be managers. I made some new friends and so I have this support system.'

The other source of Jane's anxiety and lack of confidence following her promotion was compiling written reports. 'I've always had a bit of a chip on my shoulder because I didn't go to university.' She took a course.

Focusing on learning the new skills she needed had a tremendous and unexpected effect on Jane's confidence. She's decided to turn the chip on her shoulder into a dream that she can achieve: a part-time psychology degree with the Open University.

SOCIAL LIFE AND DATING

In a world where most communication happens online, offline can be scary. Whether it's networking as part of a job, going to parties and not knowing anyone, or feeling obliged to attend social events like weddings or birthday parties, being sociable can be an ordeal.

'The first goal for someone terrified of parties is to get to a party,' says Chamorro-Premuzic, 'and the second goal is to fix the problem in general. It's important to understand that most people at parties think of themselves and *hide* their anxiety.' Though most conventional advice is to fake confidence, he views this as unrealistic and even unnecessary. 'Just be low-key and nice. Have a drink to help you relax.'

There is, however, one area, where you will need to fake just a little confidence – and that's dating. Chamorro-Premuzic (who was a matchmaker on the TV show *Dating in the Dark*) advises not revealing your insecurities in the early stages of dating and striking a balance between flirting – making the other person feel good – and treating dating like a job interview. 'Highlight what's good about you on a good day. Smart people know that if there's a relationship things will be different further down the line.'

If you can view dating as part of gaining social confidence you'll find that you'll be in less of a state. We want to encourage you to approach dating in terms of making connections with other people. See the advice on social situations and tackle dating in the same way. Find an online dating site that suits you (yes, you may have to try a few, that's normal, even for confident daters). Rather than wait to be contacted, try to be proactive – just a little. Look at profiles, say hi, send a wink. If you can think of dates in terms of half-hour coffees and a new situation to master, you'll find that after the first few they'll no longer be an ordeal. If online dating is too daunting then take a course or join some sort of group activity where suggesting a coffee during a break is part of learning together. All this builds your social confidence.

All the experts agree that repetition slowly helps to develop a good feeling, and they all point out that hugely successful people, including

CEOs and celebrities, are reserved and have to learn to develop strategies for handling parties and social situations. It's all about going to a party (or a date, or a networking event) even for just half an hour and being oneself.

ANNIE ASHDOWN ON SURVIVING SOCIAL SITUATIONS

- *'Yes, it might be awful. Stay 20 minutes instead of 30: next time it might be better.*
- *Instead of thinking 'oh God I'm nervous' change the thought to: lots of people here are probably nervous.*
- *Ask yourself: how can I do this differently? Can I make someone laugh? Can I inspire or motivate someone and somehow be of service?*
- *Look for someone else who is standing alone awkwardly. Go over and say "I'm so nervous at these things".'*

NIKI FLACKS ON DEVELOPING BODY–BRAIN COMMUNICATION

'Superficial body language advice can feel unnatural and ridiculous. But there are ways we can use the body to stop us feeling more nervous. This isn't about being fake but setting up your body in an optimum way. These tips from Flacks are based on a combination of her acting and neuroscience expertise and are based on 'talking' to the brain through your body. You can adapt this advice also to public speaking, job interviews, dating, and any social situation:

- *As soon as you arrive, head to the toilets, go into a cubicle and close the door. Throw your arms over your head, wiggle your body, take a deep breath, move your hands away from your body and make a big smile. When you go out into the party you will feel expanded, like you want to take up more space. This will make you look confident.*

- *When you go to the bar for a drink, stand further away from the bar so you have to reach for the glass. This will help you avoid clutching your arms to your body and hunching your shoulders.*
- *Imagine you have wings attached to your back so that your chest opens up wide and your shoulders relax back. This helps to stop your mind going 'Oh I'm ugly, oh I'm not thin enough'.*
- *Women – be aware of your bag – avoid clutching it tight at your hip or tight under your armpit.*
- *Every time you feel nervous, go back to the toilets into a cubicle and do a big wriggle. When you come out you'll look flushed and feel energetic.'*

REAL PEOPLE

"Miracles do happen" – John

John believed his fear of social situations was pathological and impossible to cure. The intelligent 31-year-old surveyor was living with his parents with zero social life. 'Nobody ever made an effort to speak to me and that was proof I was rubbish. I was the one no one wanted to get stuck sitting next to in a family social scenario or a work thing.'

Taking a course in art history, however, turned out to be life-changing.

'I never bothered going for coffee or drinks with the others. A couple of people started making a point of asking me to join them. It was my default setting to just say no.

During the breaks the tutor began to chat to me. A question here, a question there, then I forgot myself and started chatting too. The first turning point was one of my classmates staying behind in the break, and me having a chat with her and the tutor. I actually made them laugh. I went home elated. I could do it. Very slowly I came out of my shell.

By the end of the 12-week course I made it to the pub with the whole group. I'm never going to be the life and soul of a party, but I'm not a bore and slowly I'm getting better at small talk. And, I have a fiancée who was a classmate from that course. She was very patient as we slowly became friends after the course. Our first date was a non-date going to an art gallery on a Saturday afternoon. It wasn't a disaster. Even I could see she was so happy being with me. I totally surprised myself and asked her out for dinner. Six months later I proposed on the Eiffel Tower. Yeah, miracles do happen.'

BODY-IMAGE LIFE

66 If you pay attention to your body, eventually you will develop the sense of who you are and what works for you. 99

Dr Nitasha Buldeo, research scientist

It's all very well knowing that you need to find beauty from within, accept who you are and see the beauty in you, but the reality isn't so straightforward is it? First you need to really get behind what's going on in your head about your looks. Whether you're a man feeling under pressure to have a six-pack or a woman desperate to be slim, whether you're self-conscious because you're going bald or have acquired terrible wrinkles, it's essential to figure out what's really happening, why and how this affects your confidence.

Do you feel others are really judging you or are you judging yourself? What makes you feel good about how you look and what is a cover up for feeling bad? Differentiating between what feels good and what is a cover up for insecurities in particular takes time and self-awareness. Even when covering up insecurities there's the challenge of figuring out whether it makes that insecurity worse or gets rid of it.

So how do you know whether a beauty treatment or a diet or an exercise programme is the right side of good, whether you're caving in to pressure, or becoming addicted to a false reality of you? We all know someone who is overdoing the Botox or the body building and we don't believe that someone's claims of feeling good, so how do you know your own pursuit of looking the best you can is healthy?

Going back to the definitions of confidence, and in particular how confidence in the body feels (compared to over-confidence), is the answer: calm plus a little excited (compared to an increased heart rate, the need for alcohol or sugar or something to pep us up, and the need for attention).

Given that we live in a society obsessed with anti-ageing and perfect bodies, it's important to be gentle with ourselves as developing confidence in this area is particularly difficult. As Ashdown points out, cosmetic surgery has become almost a religion and it's not just women who are trying to stay ahead of the ageing process. 'This is a results-oriented and a youth-obsessed culture,' says Ashdown. 'So many of my clients dread getting older and lack confidence in the way they look. Many have facial surgery and I have no issue with that but it's a pity more don't opt for soul surgery. Perfectionism has become an epidemic in the 21st century.'

ANNIE ASHDOWN ON DEVELOPING HEALTHY BODY-IMAGE

- *'We know that lots of celebrities have bodies with no fat: but do we know whether they are enjoying life and laughing, or struggling with addictions and depression?*
- *If all we see is glossy and perfect this robs us of our confidence. A quiet inner confidence will help you win every time over what you look like and what size you are. Start to look beyond the veneer.*
- *A natural look is always sexier because it's closer to who we are. Finding your natural look is the route to real confidence in your looks.*
- *Stop seeing who you were, or who you want to be, or who you think you ought to be. See who you are right here, right now. Master the art of self-acceptance. Once you embrace your flaws, no one can ever hold them against you – that's a powerful place to get to.*
- *If you are in your 40s/50s, keep remembering you will be hugely alluring and seen as desirable when you are comfortable in yourself about who you are.*
- *If you're suffering hugely from low self-esteem about your looks, throw away and stop buying the glossy magazines that feed your feelings of inadequacy. So many images are photoshopped, so don't get insecure over the illusion of perfection – it doesn't exist.*
- *Stop watching all reality TV shows with their unreal versions of beauty.*
- *Real sexiness means having a sense of ease, comfort and self-acceptance. Instead of that ideal image of sexiness, focus on developing wisdom, intelligence and experience – this combination is sexy.'*

REAL PEOPLE

"A blow-dry changes my behaviour" *– Maxine*

Maxine is a highly qualified and successful gallery owner with an enviable lifestyle, travelling regularly for work and for pleasure. She looks a decade younger than 45 and manages to strike the right balance of groomed and sophisticated with effortless and laid-back ease. She doesn't follow fashion, yet she looks like she could step into the editor of *Vogue's* Manolo's – if she wasn't wearing a new, and far more interesting, designer shoe. When she confesses that she has her off-days about her weight, it's not really a surprise because she's also self-aware and articulate about her emotions. But what is a surprise is her revelation that a blow-dry can make a huge difference to her confidence when she goes into a meeting.

'When my hair is blow dried I feel good and that can outweigh how I feel about my weight and myself,' says Maxine. 'There may be no logic, but a blow-dry changes my behaviour. I've spent some time on myself for a start and that feels good. Because I feel good I really do behave differently. I'm not defensive about my choices, so if someone questions the artists I've chosen or my valuations I don't have a voice inside my head going "oh God maybe you made a mistake". Because I don't have those voices in my head I know my face doesn't tense up; I don't start frowning, and because I don't start frowning I don't start thinking "oh God I'm frowning, now the lines on my face look worse, oh God my jowls, oh God I look awful". I don't get into the spiral of "oh I'm too old to do this now, oh the art world is full of younger people, oh what am doing here, I'm useless".'

179

We've often advised you to take the focus away from you. By trying out the confidence boosters throughout, being aware of confidence robbers (Chapter 6) and developing our confidence building habits (Chapter 9), you're likely to find that you divert your mind away from your insecurities, whether these are about getting through a bad day at work or your looks. It's worth remembering that our experts are leaders in their fields and that these are not just helpful suggestions but tried and tested methods. Of course we are aware that not everything resonates with everyone, but we hope there is enough here for you to pick something manageable. Do return to this section and refresh your memory. Start with whatever feels easiest and see what a difference that makes.

ASK YOURSELF

Q The area in my life I want to tackle first is ....?

Q The area in my life I am most confident in is ....?

Q I am brave enough to try ....?

Q Step by step I know I need to work on ....?

Q I am so excited that finally I will ....?

WHAT NEXT?

We hope that at the very least you are smiling at this point and feeling confident about your ability to develop confidence. Note that we're not saying 'find' confidence or 'be confident' or 'act' confident. We've used the word 'develop' because it's a process. We all have the innate ability as human beings to master new situations, and that's confidence. So we hope this has erased any doubts in your mind that you have a problem. So what next? Well, you will be deciding what you want to master in your life and designing the process of doing so.

Our aim has been to help you be your own analyst and coach with lots of questions and tests for you to get to know yourself in relation to confidence, with the help of our experts as well as the latest research.

You may have read through the book systematically, answering all the questions and completing the tests, and proceeding slowly. Or you may have raced through to get an overview. Or maybe you simply dipped in and out according to what you felt you needed.

We don't believe in formulas so we're not going to dictate what you should do next other than to urge that you do something that resonates with *you*. And *do* something every day. Real confidence isn't something you can pick up when you consider that you need it. Real confidence comes from within so if it's going to be real you need to be connecting with yourself on a daily basis. That's the reason faking confidence doesn't work – it's a persona that isn't you.

We've given you lots to think about and lots of advice. Now it's time to translate thinking into doing. We wish you all the best. Do let us know about your unique real journey.

ABOUT PSYCHOLOGIES
MAGAZINE

Psychologies is a magazine read by those who want to lead a fulfilling life, who want to live a life on their own terms, however they choose to define it. *Psychologies* helps you discover what 'life success' looks like for you – from the inside out.

We're on a mission to find out from the best experts and latest research in psychology how we can all lead happier and more fulfilling lives. *Psychologies* is not about striving to do more but rather finding ways to BE more. Who are you? And what do you really want? These are questions we're always asking ourselves. *Psychologies* magazine is about being the best you, and we mean being in an active way: becoming the best you can be, the happiest and the most fulfilled you.

We focus on helping you understand yourself and the world around you, by gathering the latest, most compelling thinking and translating it into practical wisdom that can support you as you create the life that works for you.

Real Confidence is written by Lorna V, a prolific journalist who has written for everyone from *Cosmopolitan* to the *Sunday Times* and is one of *Psychologies'* favourite writers. Why? Not only is she a great writer who knows how to ask exactly the right questions, she's also comfortable interviewing absolutely anyone from gangsters to gurus, from the late Alexander McQueen to Nigella. But most of all she enjoys asking questions about how we can change the way we are in order to be who we really are. She really does live the *Psychologies* strap-line 'your life, your way'. She has been shortlisted for the Verity Bargate theatre award and recently decided to embark on her secret dream to act. She is currently developing a one-woman play as a writer and actor.

www.LornaV.com @LornaVwriter

REFERENCES

CHAPTER 1

1. University of Wisconsin-Madison. 'Facebook profiles raise users' self-esteem and affect behavior.' ScienceDaily. ScienceDaily, 31 May 2013. <www.sciencedaily.com/releases/2013/05/130531114725.htm>.
2. Taylor & Francis. 'Does Facebook affect our self-esteem, sense of belonging?' ScienceDaily. ScienceDaily, 8 May 2014. <www.sciencedaily.com/releases/2014/05/140508095456.htm>.
3. 'Perceived self-efficacy is defined as people's beliefs about their capabilities to produce designated levels of performance that exercise influence over events that affect their lives.' A. Bandura. 1994. Self-efficacy. In V. S.Ramachaudran (Ed.), *Encyclopedia of Human Behavior* (Vol. 4, pp. 71–81). New York: Academic Press. (Reprinted in H. Friedman [Ed.] (1998), *Encyclopedia of Mental Health*. San Diego: Academic Press).

CHAPTER 4

1. University at Buffalo. 'Who am I? New study links early family experiences, self-esteem with self-clarity.' ScienceDaily. ScienceDaily, 9 March 2015. <www.sciencedaily.com/releases/2015/03/150309093301.htm>.
2. Professor Robert Plomin, Institute of Psychiatry, King's College London. http://www.kcl.ac.uk/ioppn/news/records/2009/06June/Academicself-confidence50natureand50nurture.aspx.

CHAPTER 5

1. Amy Novotny. 'Understanding our personalities requires a lesson in history.' *Monitor*, December 2008. http://www.apa.org/monitor/2008/12/kagan.aspx.

CHAPTER 6

1. Baumeister et al. 2003. 'Does self-esteem cause better performance, interpersonal success, happiness or healthier lifestyles?' *Psychological Science in the Public Interest* Vol. 4, No. 1.

CHAPTER 7

1. Concordia University. 'Boosting self-esteem prevents health problems for seniors.' ScienceDaily. ScienceDaily, 12 March 2014. <www.sciencedaily.com/releases/2014/03/140312132623.htm>.

CHAPTER 8

1. Jaye L. Derrick, Shira Gabriel, Brooke Tippin. 2008. 'Parasocial relationships and self-discrepancies: Faux relationships have benefits for low self-esteem individuals.' *Personal Relationships*, Vol 15: 261–80.
2. University of Edinburgh. 'Self-delusion is a winning survival strategy, study suggests.' ScienceDaily. ScienceDaily, 14 September 2011. <www.sciencedaily.com/releases/2011/09/110914131352.htm>.
3. Brunel University. 'Facebook status updates reveal low self-esteem and narcissism.' ScienceDaily. ScienceDaily, 21 May 2015. <www.sciencedaily.com/releases/2015/05/150521213743.htm>.
4. University at Buffalo. 'Facebook photo sharing reflects focus on female appearance.' ScienceDaily. ScienceDaily, 7 March 2011. <www.sciencedaily.com/releases/2011/03/110307124826.htm>.
5. Columbia Business School. 'Social networks may inflate self-esteem, reduce self-control.' ScienceDaily. ScienceDaily, 14 January 2013. <www.sciencedaily.com/releases/2013/01/130114133353.htm>.
6. University of California – Berkeley Haas School of Business. 'Why are people overconfident so often? It's all about social status.'

ScienceDaily. ScienceDaily, 13 August 2012. <www.sciencedaily
.com/releases/2012/08/120813130712.htm>.

7. William James. 1890. *The Principles of Psychology*. Dover
Publications; reprint edition (June 1, 1950).

8. University of Georgia. 'High self-esteem is not always what it's
cracked up to be.' ScienceDaily. ScienceDaily, 28 April 2008. <www
.sciencedaily.com/releases/2008/04/080428084235.htm>.

9. Detroy Paulhaus, P.D. Harms, M.N. Bruce, and D.C. Lysy. 2003.
'The over-claiming technique: measuring self-enhancement
independent of ability'. *Journal of Personality and Social
Psychology* Vol 84, No 4: 890–904.

CHAPTER 9

1. University of Melbourne. 'Self-confidence the secret to workplace
advancement.' ScienceDaily. ScienceDaily, 18 October 2012.
<www.sciencedaily.com/releases/2012/10/121018103214
.htm>.

2. Ohio State University. 'Body posture affects confidence
in your own thoughts, study finds.' ScienceDaily.
ScienceDaily, 5 October 2009. <www.sciencedaily.com/
releases/2009/10/091005111627.htm>

3. Amy J.C., Cuddy, Caroline A. Wilmuth, Andy J. Yap, and Dana
R. Carney. 2015. 'Preparatory power posing affects nonverbal
presence and job interview outcomes.' *Journal of Applied
Psychology* Vol. 100, No. 4: 1286–95. Dana R., Carney, Amy J.C.
Cuddy, and Andy J. Yap. 2010. 'Power posing: brief nonverbal
displays affect neuroendocrine levels and risk tolerance.'
Psychological Science Vol. 21, No. 10: 1363–68.

CHAPTER 10

1. CNRS (Délégation Paris Michel-Ange). 'Culture influences
young people's self-esteem: Fulfillment of value priorities
of other individuals important to youth.' ScienceDaily.
ScienceDaily, 24 February 2014. <www.sciencedaily.com/
releases/2014/02/140224081027.htm>.

Notes